Sandman's Advice
To The Unpopular

Sandman's Advice To The Unpopular

an
ABC
BOOK

Other Books by The Sandman

Forewords

In treading the deeps of my life, I often felt heavy with the sense of a brutal personal inadequacy. Suddenly, my soul took flight. I met the Sandman. His comely ineptitude and absurdist conversational tactics filled me to the point of brimming hope. How could I fret about my own indecency in the face of one like Sandy whose life, after all, is wrought from the energy of miserable failure? Thanks, Sandy. In all your paleness, you serve to make many feel, by contrast, mighty real. I will carry this volume always as an emotional armoury.

Sandy has asked me to reminisce. He insists our initial meeting occurred some years back at a Biennale installation in Newtown. Something to do with offal and discontent. The details elude me. I can report, however, that Sandy maintains a strong interest in conceptual art. The Australia Council can attest to this. The jolly funding factory has received and rejected at least two hundred Sandy-devised grant applications. One can only hope that justice will prevail and the key representative might of the Gemini will be felt in art-spaces everywhere.

Until that golden time when the cruel arbiters of creative worth are mere dust ... please enjoy these lambent and faintly sexual prose poems. Surely the Sandman inhabits that hitherto uncharted terrain between High Art and Newcastle.

Helen Razer

Well folks it's finally happened; Sandy has a book out and you've purchased it. Well done, it will look good on any bookself. If however you are looking through it at the bookshop, buy it now, go no further, don't try speed reading it and then putting it back on the shelf—you ought to be ashamed of yourself. Here you are with one of the great works of Australian literature in your hand and you can't decide whether to buy it or some long boring novel by an overrated British author that'll impress your friends but you'll never finish anyway.

Sure Sandy may never win the Booker Prize but he does have a bronze medallion and how many authors do you know can say that. Besides it's a good read with nice illustrations by the charming but deeply disturbed Michael Bell. There are even rumours that it might be on the Year Twelve reading list as soon as we can get that loser Shakespeare, dumped once and for all. In fact I liked it so much I even paid for my copy—well I had to, Sandy mailed all his free ones to ex-teachers who said he'd never amount to anything. I bet they feel stupid now.

Of course Sandman deserves all the success that he is presently having so much difficulty coping with. We just hope that it won't change him, although any improvement in personal hygiene would be great. So go on, be a sport and buy the book. Maybe then the bastard will give me back the twenty bucks he's owed me since 1985 (he lost a bet over which one of us could eat more green prawns).

Mikey Robins

Author's Note

Thank you for getting this far. Before you make a decision to read further, I must point out a few things and thank a few people.

This book is made up from my favourite Sandman bits on the Triple J breakfast radio show, mine hosts, Helen Razer and Mikel Robins, between 1993–5. They may not be my best bits because I'm not always a good judge of what is best, but they are my personal favourites.

Keep in mind, all the bits are written to be read aloud, by me. Therefore, it may help with your enjoyment of this book, if you were to read them aloud, yourself, at least once. Pick a piece, think of something you've lost—youth, a pet, a loved one or a partner—to give the monologue resonance, then, in a slow, dull, and monotone voice, read it out loud. If it takes about one minute thirty seconds to read one piece, then you're reading at the right speed.

I'd like to thank the following people for their help. Helen Razer, Mikel Robins, Mark Kennedy for producing the stuff for radio, the friendly staff at Triple J, Anna McAllan, Angela Moore, Paul Livingston, Glenn Butcher for the songbook, Michael Bell for his expert drawings, Claire Martin, Ray Hughes, Evelyn Abbott and Warren Coleman for the use of his talking buttocks concept.

I'd like to point out that The Sandman is the figment of someone's imagination. Any resemblance to anything or anyone real is pure coincidence.

Thank you for buying, borrowing or browsing at this book.

The end.

This book is dedicated to Lorimar and Evelyn and me.

Published by ABC Books for the
AUSTRALIAN BROADCASTING CORPORATION
GPO Box 9994 Sydney NSW 2001

First published May 1995
Reprinted May 1996
Reprinted December 1996

National Library of Australia
Cataloguing-in-Publication entry
The Sandman 1956– .
    Sandman's advice to the unpopular.

    ISBN 0 7333 0450 8.

    1. Australian wit and humour — 20th century. 2. Social
    skills — Australia — Humour. I. Australian Broadcasting
    Corporation. II. Triple J (Radio station).

302.14

Illustrated by Michael Bell
Designed by Paul Stanish
set in 10¹/₂12¹/₂pt Schneidler Old Style by
Midland Typesetters, Maryborough, Victoria
Printed and bound in Australia by
Australian Print Group, Maryborough, Victoria

5 4 3

Contents

Beware of the Two Way Crack

I choose to start the story now.

I first discovered the 'Two Way Crack' when I was boarding at the Sunstruck Guesthouse. Every morning, as I'd leave for work at the brick refractory, I'd walk past the proprietors' (a Mr Sands) half-closed bedroom door where he'd be lying in bed with his wife Conchita.

I'd take great delight from my one second of insight into their private lives through the crack between the door and the door jam. The lift I got from seeing them so vulnerable was enormous.

Five weeks this went on. Five days a week for five weeks—twenty-five seconds of private life I obtained. I discovered details like Mr Sands kissed with his mouth open while Conchita's lips were often closed white-hard with Latin emotion. Mr Sands also liked to be touched at the base of the spine which made his head rock from side to side and his tongue poke in and out.

One morning outside my room Mr Sands grabbed me from behind and pulled my shirt so hard I had trouble breathing. He growled at me like he'd had four Cerepax and two moselles. He said if I looked through the crack one more time, he'd poke my eyes out with a biro.

If you've discovered a window of opportunity, be very careful. You're vulnerable too. I'd seen into the Sands' lives but unknowingly, they'd seen into mine.

It was a Two Way Crack.

The end.

A Silent Success is a Failure

I choose to start the story now.

When Craig Ritter started catching my bus and growling at me under his breath, suddenly my name was on everybody's lips.

Craig was a legend. He once ate a seagull in front of the Commonwealth Bank in Ballina (he put it between two bits of white sliced) and now he was after me because someone had told him I'd kicked him during his fight with Saul Cassevettes at the rifle range. How could I turn this situation to my advantage without too much pain?

I put two bricks in my bag, strapped a piece of aluminimium to my forearm and caught the bus as usual. On the expressway Craig was well into his growling routine when I stood up and started pounding him. Sadly, most of my blows struck Frank Manifold in the seat behind and he'd always been kind to me in the past.

Despite being a poor puncher I was having major success because Craig was trapped in his seat and couldn't move.

Suddenly the bus stopped. The driver (Mr Norton) strode down the aisle, broke us up and threw us both onto the road. I'll never forget the bus pulling away and me being cheered by kids who'd only ever hidden my clothes and spat on me in the past.

Unfortunately I tripped on loose gravel as I bent down to pick up my bag and Craig Ritter was able to severely beat me until a guy in an EH Holden pulled over and stopped him. Nevertheless, I'd been a success in front of the others and that was all that mattered.

The end.

If You Have to Criticise a Defensive Person, Use a Beach Towel

I choose to start the story now.

I once had a Persian cat called Jackson. Every month I had to get the knots out of his fur without him scratching me. It wasn't easy. He struggled so much a giant white foam bubble formed around his mouth. The only way to ensure you weren't attacked was to wrap him in a large beach towel.

A similar technique can be used when criticising or teasing a defensive person. Like Jackson, they often bite and scratch to save face. I know.

On one particular occasion, during an Air Supply concert, a group of surf-club types tried to take my clothes off and push me onto the stage in front of the audience. I was so intimidated by surf-club boys, I hadn't been for a swim at a patrolled beach for three years. Even then I still wore denim jeans pulled high to cover a large hairy mat at the base of my spine.

I resisted all their efforts to humiliate me until they wrapped me in a large beach towel and rolled me on stage.

Thankfully, Air Supply were near the end of their lifespan so there were only 80 people in the 1000 seat auditorium.

The end.

Even in Your Darkest Hour There's a Spongy Piece of Cardboard to Lie Down and Have a Bludge On

I choose to start the story now.

Working at the steelworks is the worst job I've ever had. Not only did I weep on my way to work, there was no STD phone, a tough guy always hid my 'civvy' clothes and everybody had gourmet food in hot pots. I only ever had sandwiches bound in a type of gladwrap that could never be unlocked.

However, my demeanour changed completely after I was taken through a small door near the Hot Strip Mill by a Turkish chap. Much to my surprise there was a virtual paradise there. Banana trees, a fridge with beer, spongy cardboard to lie on, surfboards to hire, fake doctor's certificates, a barbecue area and even a tailor who could do simple alterations at short notice.

The older workers would even stay after their shifts had finished because they felt the atmosphere was better than at their respective homes. The only drag was a group of Fitters who sang Bee Gees' songs in unison (a minor quibble).

I still weep on my way to work but I now know that even in the darkest hellhole there's a piece of spongy cardboard to lie down and have a bludge on.

The end.

If You Intend to Exhilarate a Person, Make Sure You Have the Strength of Two People

I choose to start the story now.

At a barbecue some of the men were demonstrating feats of strength in front of a small but very attentive crowd. One chap called Arthur swung Skye Silisbury around his head (Skye is a not a slight woman either). Another man lifted a dining chair with a child on it using just the back right-hand leg of the chair and one arm. Another man shifted a huge pile of blue metal form one side of the yard to the other in under four minutes.

After they were finished and the crowd had dispersed, I went over to Skye and asked her if I could swing her around like Arthur had. The moment I grabbed her forearms and felt her weight I knew the task was beyond me. I got started all right, but I couldn't consistently keep Skye off the ground. I took the skin off her elbow and forehead and when she landed the impact also ripped her dress. She was stunned and bleeding as she lay motionless on the cement. I was numb and worried. So I did what our family has always done when the going gets tough—I ran.

If you intend to exhilarate someone, make sure you have the strength of two. And don't swing people round your head while standing on cement either.

The end.

If You're Inhibited, You Need Something or Someone You Can Be Totally Free With

I choose to start the story now.

For some people emotional freedom may be found in their family, a relationship, or even a dog that recognises your whistle. For me, it's my bathroom. I feel totally uninhibited in my bathroom because I know it and trust it.

I know my wooden toilet seat will not leave a red ring on my bottom if I sit with my weight forward. I know if I lie on the tiles when I'm 'pissy pants' it makes me feel better. I know if I curl my toes inwards then it's tolerable to walk on the tiles without socks in winter. I know that if my toothbrush falls in between the sink and the wall I can get it out with the piece of cane that holds the fern up straight. I know when sunlight hits the wall during August it gives off a yellow light which makes me feel like I'm in Egypt.

I can't hug it like a parent or borrow money from it like I could a human friend, but I'm glad I have my bathroom.

There are four things I like in life: fresh sheets on my bed, my sweets arriving no later than four minutes after my main meal, seeing someone miss out on something they desperately want and two uninterrupted 20-minute stints in my bathroom so I can be myself for just under an hour each day.

My bathroom is my best friend.

The end.

A Tiger Suit Can Help Overcome Shyness

I choose to start the story now.

One of the problems with being shy is the inability to be yourself in public. The one exception to this rule for me was when I worked as Terry the Tiger for B & L Motors.

Every Thursday night, after I'd washed the cars and been called shag by the Sales Manager, I'd slip on the tiger suit (known as Terry) and give out pamphlets. Being hidden inside that suit gave me such a feeling of freedom, and because the fur was both inside and out I felt like I was getting hugged by my parents.

Then one night my freedom was taken away when I was spat on by four guys in a red Cortina. As I bent

over to wipe their spit of my thighs, a child sneaked
up behind me and kicked me right in the anus—
which was uncovered so you didn't have to take the
suit off to go to the toilet (time is money in the car
industry)—and I farted very loudly.

The mother of the child complained to the
Manager. She thought I'd made the sound with my
mouth and I was holding my bottom and thrusting
my pelvis out just to be rude.

If I could've taken that tiger suit with me (after I
was sacked) I could've been myself more often. I'd
have been hot in summer but I'd have held down
more jobs.

The end.

It's Important to Have Authentic Purpose

I choose to start the story now.

During my early twenties I was very unpopular. I had a few friends but they were constantly punched for no reason. This lack of popularity culminated for me when I was king-hit at a local Leagues Club for pretending to be Allan Border to a group of nurses from Tumut. It was obvious I needed my own purpose in life. I decided I should mine the inside out of the old brick rifle range near my house with a crowbar.

Almost immediately, I reaped the benefits of having this as my main purpose in life. Everybody in the area started talking about me. Even when I passed the Croatians who gathered near the TAB I knew they were saying, in their own language, 'There goes the chap who mined the inside out of the old brick rifle range with a crowbar'. I don't speak Croatian but I can read a face.

Sadly, the rifle range fell down after a huge electric storm one day, killing two expensive greyhounds and smashing the arm of their owner Nick the Dip. This resulted in me being hit over the head with a shotgun in the car park of the Leagues Club and receiving 22 stitches.

If the purpose is hollow, the confidence is false.

The end.

A Piece of Cucumber Can Create Interest Where Originally There Was None

I choose to start the story now.

Normally when I make eye contact with someone they look away and I pick my teeth and that's it. However, one night a strong woman from across a crowded room kept looking at me. She was wearing an apricot cardigan with a name tag pinned on it. I think it said 'Nicole'.

I must have looked up on six occasions and every time I did we made eye contact with each other. I was so excited I got the giggles, my eyes started watering and I struggled with the sensation that I was about to sneeze. I always get hay fever when I'm anxious.

As I departed the hotel—having had rapport with a strong contemporary woman called Nicole—two sailors stopped me and said I had a piece of cucumber stuck to my neck.

I felt around my hairline, and sure enough, there was a small ring of cucumber stuck to my neck. This did put a seed of doubt in my mind. Was Nicole interested in me or was she staring at the cucumber?

After some initial disappointment I decided I didn't care. I'd felt wanted and attractive for over an hour and that's all that mattered.

Now a ring of cucumber features regularly in my social rituals.

The end.

Ring Friends Before Visiting. Otherwise You Could Be Shocked

I choose to start the story now.

I should not have visited Don without calling him first.

When I got to Don's house I knocked on his front door. Even though no one answered I decided to try round the back because I could hear music coming from inside the house. I cautiously went up the side and sure enough there he was, in the backyard, lying naked, in a very strange way, on the path that led to his clothes line.

I went over to him. There were signs of life. His eyes were rotating and his tongue was going in and out, but he didn't seem to register my presence at all. Even when I yelled out 'Don' several times, he didn't move. His behaviour was so strange that I sneaked away and pushed my Gemini down the street so he couldn't hear the familiar sound of my engine starting.

As I drove off I remembered how Don used to trap flies in his Perkins Paste jar at school. His title pages were always lumpy. And now here he was looking so reptilian. It was as if he was lying on the path trying to warm his blood like a lizard would. I would've rather not seen this private side of Don.

If I'd rung first, I would not have been disappointed.

The end.

Don't Try Too Hard to Impress

I choose to start the story now.

I arrived at a new school on the same day as a boy called Toby Chee. It's interesting to see how we both tried a different approach to winning approval.

I was quiet. A closed door creates interest. It was two months before anyone even knew my first name.

Toby, on the other hand, was very loud. By day two he was already going 'Arh Arh' like a pirate when he was spoken to. On day three, he was waving an imaginary cutlass about to complement his pirate image.

Day four (late night shopping), everyone went to the Mall to hang out. I wasn't allowed to see the city at night so I didn't go, but apparently Toby arrived dressed as a pirate and he'd customised his Ford Escort to look like a pirate ship as well. Protruding from the centre of his van was a 16 foot cedar mast, complete with a functional crow's nest, a tiny quarterdeck at the back and ship's wheel where he stood and steered from.

Toby only got 40 metres up the street when the
mast struck overhead powerlines. Not only was he
electrocuted, which caused him to soil his pants, he
lost his licence, got sued by the Council and was
declared 'king dweeb' by the cool group who hung at
Pemberton's Light and Sound in their wetsuits.

Toby had tried too hard to impress. Besides, pirates
are naff. Always have been, always will be. For
example, Adam Ant.

The end.

The Day I Chose Two Coloured Pencils Over My Team-mates

I choose to start the story now.

There're 13 players in a Rugby League team plus reserves. The job of occupying number 14 and 15 in my team always went to Ken Sorenson and myself. Even if there was an injury our coach would play one short rather than send Ken or myself on to play. That suited me because I'm allergic to adrenalin. It makes my right eye go puffy. Besides, the most important part of the game for me was the two hours afterwards.

After every game I'd always stay in my gear and dive in some mud to make it look like I'd been involved. Then I'd change my number 15 to a 7 with water soluble neo magic pen and sit on the toilet with a coloured pencil in each hand. With arms outstretched and pencils whirring in front of my eyes (so they looked like legs running), I'd re-commentate our game with me playing the major part.

One day my imaginary life was threatened when the coach needed me to play. Feeling my eye swelling up as I jogged onto the paddock, I had to make a snap decision. So I did. I ran straight across the field to the railway station and got the train home.

I didn't want reality to ruin my rich imaginary life in the toilet with two pencils and a neo magically altered jersey.

The end.

Before Reading Further, Get to Know Sandman Better

Sandman, what did your parents want you to be?

A sales rep.

What is your favourite food?
Sauce.

What's the best thing you've ever done?

Shaved a space in between my eyebrows.

What's the biggest mistake you've ever made?

Confusing brake fluid with Blackberry Nip.

What's your best feature?

I always sleep eight hours.

Favourite animals?

The currawong—it has a communal sense that's quite superb—and the greyhound, because it can actually catch seagulls at the beach.

What's your vision for the future?

That I'll be more handsome with age.

What's your biggest fear?

That I'll be a success. Or doing a poo in someone else's toilet.

Worst habit?

Picking my nose and rubbing it in my eyes!

Hobbies?

Eavesdropping.

What's your earliest memory?

Having a dry mouth and needing a drink of water.

What words might other people use to describe you?

'Nevertheless' and 'anyway'.

What's your idea of extravagance?

Leaving a light on when I go out.

What's your favourite word?

'Champion'.

What words do you most overuse?

'Stop' and 'it'.

What do you dislike about yourself most?

My body and my face.

What were your parents going to call you if you were a girl?

Prudence.

What's the one thing you want most in life?

A partner.

How would you like to be remembered?

As someone with a partner.

If You're Desperate Enough, You Will Belong

I choose to start the story now.

I couldn't understand Greg's willingness to fight Brainiac. Greg was blond and handsome, whereas Brainiac was 6 foot 2 inches, ugly, unbeaten in street fights and because of the fear factor the most popular guy in our area.

The fight itself was over a misunderstanding that occurred when the lights went out at a soccer presentation night. Greg allegedly said something nasty about Brainiac's girlfriend. Next thing Greg was picked and waiting behind the boatshed for Brainiac to arrive.

It was a quick fight. Brainiac simply king-hit Greg while he was taking his parka off. I went over to Greg (I didn't go straight away because I didn't want to be seen as his friend in front of the others), and he looked up at me, his nose resting on his face.

'Is it broken?' he said excitedly.

'Do you usually wear your nose on the right side of your face?' I replied.

We spent the rest of that night in my Gemini, visiting the homes of all the leaders in the different social scenes so Greg could show them his nose.

That night Greg was accepted into the Bank Corner Boys. If you're desperate enough, you shall belong.

The end.

Men Compare Sporting Injuries Rather than Emotional Scars

I choose to start the story now.

I was desperate to belong to the peer group that met on the grassed area at the beach. They always wore colourful sporting gear, had short haircuts and a host of niggling injuries they'd compare every Monday.

They'd start by pulling up their trouser legs to see who had the worst bruising on their shins. Eventually they'd move on to the facial area where swollen lips, bruised facial tissue, bent noses and stitches got big prizes.

The reason I wanted to join them was that they never seemed to reveal themselves emotionally. Instead of discussing fears, desires or emotional hurt they compared sporting injures, which, at the time, seemed a less painful option than revealing the truth about yourself. I decided I had to bite the bullet, get some injuries and see if I could join them.

The next Sunday I rolled down a slope covered with blackberry bushes to get some appropriate lacerations and I hit my nose with the side of a ruler several times to look nasally competitive.

While doing this I found I had a very low tolerance to physical pain. I decided it was less painful telling the truth. Also, when you're unpopular it's better to keep your looks.

The end.

Pride in Your Jersey

I choose to start the story now.

It was grand final week and the boys were all fired up by our coach's speech about pride in your jersey. Expecially the bit when he threw an adjustable spanner through the change room window to emphasise a point. As a tribute to the coach we all pledged not to take our jerseys off until after the game.

Tony Stillman was so fired up by the coach that he ate a live chicken sandwich. Brainiac hopped out of a moving vehicle. Rick drank brake fluid and was sick all over a table at the Pizza Hut. And our centres, Slug and Cypherman, stole a bus and drove to Cooma.

On the Saturday we gathered at the ground for the big day. Tony Stillman had been arrested for cruelty to animals, so he was out. Brainiac had scraped part of his face off diving out of the moving car and was ruled unfit. Rick was on the critical list, having burnt the lining off his stomach drinking brake fluid. Slug and Cypherman both had terrible carpet burns on their buttocks from dragging each other up and down a hotel corridor (naked) in Cooma and couldn't walk properly.

The coach glared at me.

'Haven't you got any pride in your jersey? Those boys bled for each other and you've got the gall to turn up without an injury.'

I said, 'I've got strict parents and I had to go home early.'

The end.

Derek–The 20-minute Wonder God

I choose to start the story now.

I'll never forget the night Derek kicked in the door of a Fellowship van in Coolangatta.

As Derek pounded the van he was like a man possessed—yelling after every blow and swearing at the top of his voice. By the time he'd finished there was blood on his knuckles, his shirt was hanging off his body and he'd drawn quite a crowd. Mostly teary Fellowship types dressed in yellow T-shirts, Key Man jeans and Roman sandals.

It was the first time anyone had seen Derek make such a big contribution to our social scene. To mark the occasion we carried him shoulder high through the Mall, but because Derek was plump we got tired quickly and had to put him down near the fountain.

At the very same moment, the boys saw a group of girls go into a disco. Ironically, the dress regulations at the disco specified a shirt and Derek didn't have a proper shirt any more so he couldn't get in. He didn't seem to mind. He was more than happy with his night.

In fact, the only sour note occurred as the boys went inside the venue. The moment they disappeared Derek vomited onto an old retread that was about 2 metres away. They missed his record breaking vomit.

The end.

The Day I Discovered Why I Was a Test Pilot for All Types of Student Torture

I choose to start the story now.

Our family were driving to Narooma to see 'fake' Aunty Coral. Her kelpie Amigo was going to sing 'Hey Jude' at the school fete. In our hearts we knew it would be just barking, but she was our family's best friend and she'd done it tough since her husband was caught stealing crates of cordial from a private school.

We'd stopped for lunch in Ulladulla. I'd ordered four hamburgers to see if I could eat that many. I always set challenges for myself on car trips. My mother went off to leave a message on the answering machine for our cat Alice so she wouldn't feel abandoned. Then I looked at Dad, who was gasping for air. His burger had stuck in his throat because someone was staring at him. Then it hit me. It wasn't just Coral, all our family and friends were odd. It was hereditary.

Suddenly I knew why I was constantly hit with a wet tennis ball and preyed upon for no apparent reason at school.

That trip was a revelation. Dad even taught me how not to cry when I was being flicked with a beach towel rolled up like a kangaroo's tail.

Thank you Ulladulla for making our family closer.

The end.

A Closed Door Creates Interest

I choose to start the story now.

A few years ago, as I was untying a friend who was chained nude to a set of traffic lights in the main street, I noticed a crowd standing five deep around the display windows of a large department store. It was still 15 minutes before opening time.

The reason for the crowd was that the windows of the store were covered with brown paper except for a few small peepholes which people were actually fighting over. I remember thinking to myself, yes, a closed door creates interest. I should apply this principle at the cricket presentation this evening.

That night I was a closed door—aloof and arrogant. It worked so well that by 11.30 I had all these people interested in me.

At times they were gathered five deep but, unfortunately, I had nothing to say. So I did what I always do when I can't think of anything to say—I pulled down my pants. I was subsequently punched in the temple by an irate father who had his young daughter with him.

When the store opened, exactly the same thing happened. Inside the shop it was just the same old stock so the people moved off to watch some students from a local high school do jazz aerobics in the Mall.

Don't make the same mistake as the store and I did. Have something inside. Even if it's cheap or stolen.

The end.

Spontaneous Acts Have a Short Life Span

I choose to start the story now.

I felt so tall when I suggested to my friends that we all stop what we're doing and go to the Snowy. It was 10.05 on a Thursday night. I'd had nine vodkas and orange and I felt like I could change the world.

At first my friends praised my sense of spontaneity, but as we drove around getting blankets everyone sobered up and the idea of going to the Snowy started to seem like a chore. By the time we hit the road it was only Craig Melvee and myself in the Gemini, and he was too drunk to realise what he was doing.

It was at Jindabyne, when I slipped on some icy steps in ugh boots and split my eye open, that I began to realise the glow from a spontaneous act only lasts a couple of hours. This view was reinforced when Craig and I discovered blankets and a car heater did not provide sufficient warmth against the coldness of Smiggins Hole.

On the way home Craig spontaneously put the car into reverse doing 110 k. After that, every time I changed into second gear the horn came on.

Then he unexpectedly yelled at some guys with tattoos at a set of traffic lights in Sutherland. The Gemini stalled on take-off and we were both beaten to a pulp in a park near the railway station.

It was a spontaneous yet truly poor holiday.

The end.

It's Easier to Love Something that Reminds You of Yourself

I choose to start the story now.

I've had a few pets but I've always been disappointed with them because they've not reflected my own habits.

I once had a budgie called Peter who could talk but he'd only ever say my neighbours' Christian names. He just made a coughing sound whenever he looked at me. I pride myself on my ability to remember names. I can often recall what people were wearing, too. It's important to remember banal things.

I also had a cat called Jackson whose breath was so bad he left a brown stain on the wall where his rug used to be. He had a habit of snuggling in with me every morning. It got so bad that I had to

leave a bucket by the bed because his breath would make me gag. I never hug anyone (I'm frightened by demonstrative types), so Jackson and I never bonded.

Now I have a dog. Not a puppy because I'm not interested in something with a future. He's a kelpie-cattle dog cross and I call him 'The Tight Piece of Work'. He doesn't come when I call, if you make an unexpected movement he barks, his ears are constantly pricked up as if he's suspicious, he's so highly strung that he walks one inch above the ground and no other dogs ever warm to him. If he was a human he'd be a bed pumper.

I love The Tight Piece of Work because he reminds me of me.

The end.

Be Careful When Changing Houses: In Between Houses You're Vulnerable

I choose to start the story now.

When you live somewhere for a while you tend to develop patterns of behaviour to reduce your level of vulnerability.

When I moved house recently I was tense because I was in between patterns. I didn't know how to act in my new area.

For example, the road in front of my new house was quite wide. When a car was approaching, did I run or walk to cross? If I ran, I looked eager. If I walked, I was arrogant. I just didn't know what the done thing was.

My neighbours still kept in touch with the people who lived in the house before. When I bagged the padded toilet seat they left behind (I told my neighbour it felt like you were sitting on a snake when you did a poo), I could easily have been saying the wrong thing.

The one positive thing about being 'in between houses' is that while you're packing up the old house you find things you forgot you had.

For instance, I found a set of pink decorative masks I got in Bali. If I wore them when I went out, my neighbours found it very hard to establish who actually lived at my house. If I embarrassed myself in the local area, it didn't have ongoing ramifications.

I could have been anyone underneath those bright decorative masks from Bali.

The end.

A Tennis Ball Can Be a Temporary Substitute for Compassion

I choose to start the story now.

As Charlie lay on the footpath, Pam and I were numb. Obviously an egg thrown from a speeding vehicle hurts, especially if it catches you directly in the eye, but Charlie was virtually convulsing as he yelled, 'I can't see! I can't see!'

His hysterical screaming attracted some nearby residents, who gathered around Charlie, Pam and myself. The sight of blood coming from inside Charlie's eye was quite disturbing, and it made Pam vomit through her hand. At that point, I sensed the eyes of the crowd shift from Charlie, to Pam, then to me. I could tell they were thinking, 'Show him some compassion. Put your arm around him'.

Then I remembered I had a tennis ball in my pocket. So I got it out and started throwing it to Charlie, trying to make him catch it, and saying well done if he did. I'm good at distracting people who are sulking. Although Charlie wasn't really sulking. He was in shock.

I know it may seem a little odd, throwing a tennis ball to a person haemorrhaging from the eyes, but like most people, I feel more comfortable when I've got something to do.

I moved cities six weeks after that incident anyway.

The end.

I Hate Sunny Days

I choose to start the story now.

I'm so angry when I wake up and the sun is
shining. It means I have too many decisions to make.
Should I go outside? Should I take a jumper in case
there's a southerly change? Should I do something
physical that takes advantage of the warm
conditions? Sunny days make me flustered and
snappy.

On the other hand, rainy days make me feel secure
and free. When it rains there's no point in going
outside. There is very little for me to decide except to
cancel all my plans and remember I have exactly four
minutes to make the toilet after my first coffee in the
morning.

Somethings never change.

The end.

Eat Fast: It's Good to Finish First at Something

I choose to start the story now.

Whenever you finish first at something, even if it's just your dinner, someone will say 'Gee you were quick', and that's valuable seconds of attention.

When it came to eating fast, my father was never beaten. His 'conveyor belt custard-eating technique' is still remembered to this very day.

Ideally, his custard bowl was slipped straight into where his dinner plate was. With dessert spoon in hand, a constant whirring motion ensured his custard got from spoon to mouth in a blur to rival that of a hummingbird's wings. Whenever we had custard for dessert, our neighbours would come over to watch. Or at least ring to find out how fast he went.

If anyone ate faster than him, he could step up a gear too. He'd simply visualise a second set of teeth in his stomach which allowed him to eat and swallow without chewing.

Eating fast does have a by-product—fat. And excess fat can create insecurities. Keep in mind that this can be used in a confessional-style film project or a book of monologues later in your life.

If you do find being overweight a drag, just lose the weight quickly. People will praise you for it and you'll have a surplus of stretched skin to use for party tricks too.

The end.

Stand Up
In Pressure Situations

I choose to start the story now.

At my end of year TAFE party, Gail, a mature age student, sat on my lap, and played with a calcified pointy bit on the top of my left ear. Even though my legs started to hurt after ten minutes, I didn't say anything to her because it felt like we were having an affair. Each little movement of Gail's bottom revealed a new sensation for me. A bit like the role of spices in a superior curry.

I kept my breathing shallow, in case I had bad breath, and my eyes closed, as much as humanly possible, so she might notice that I had very long eyelashes.

After half an hour I began to experience severe pain. Her buttocks were pressing on my bladder, I had pins and needles in the lower half of my body and I was dizzy from panting.

After forty minutes I was just about to ask her to move, when Gail said, 'Do you want to go now?' 'We could stop somewhere for hello kisses'. She kissed me on the forehead and whispered, 'Hello', and I shivered in anticipation of more.

However, when she stood up, and said, 'Let's go swarthy,' I couldn't move. My legs were completely numb. All I could do was drop off the chair and wet myself. I suspect Gail was after someone who was better under pressure than me.

Next time I see her I'll stand up.

The end.

Marriage Can Isolate Couples

I choose to start the story now.

During my holidays I went camping with a married couple. We hired a big tent as a mess hall plus two three-person tents for sleeping purposes. The only rule was, if their tent flap was down I was not to disturb them. It meant they were having sex.

Their flap was down six or seven times a day, which meant I was in the mess tent for up to five hours a day by myself. My feeling of frustration was also heightened by six days of constant rain. That meant the married couple spent even more time inside their tent with the flap down because there was nothing else for them to do.

The other side effect, of the torrential rain, was that it flushed out plague proportions of Funnel Web spiders, which in turn caused total evacuation of the camping area.

I had a nasty argument with one of the Rangers when he tried moving us on. 'You can't disturb the people in the other tent because their flap is down. They're having sex'.

By the time they emerged, from their tent of constant lovemaking, there was a carpet of Funnel Webs throughout the camping ground. Not to mention a ute full of angry Rangers waiting for them at the entrance. The married couple were unaware of any developments outside their own world.

The end.

Uncle Nev, Two Bits of Rope and a Wasp's Nest

I choose to start the story now.

I'd like to show how two gimmicks helped a person with a difficult personality be warmly remembered.

I worshipped my Uncle Nev because he'd always do a magic trick with two pieces of rope and show me the wasp's nest that was attached to a light fitting in his backyard whenever I visited. Simple one-on-one situations that have stayed with me to this day.

FIGURE 58

Later in life, when I discovered Uncle Nev ran an illegal time-share business in a wine bar called the Bamboo Room, I still had a soft spot for him. Likewise when I heard he made his second wife run down a dirt track, with no shoes on and holding a brick above her head, after he'd caught her smoking.

FIGURE 59

Even when I was told he forced his dog to eat paspalum and that he once squashed a hot pie in a neighbour's face for leaving oil on his drive. I still had that soft spot for him.

And when I discovered his neighbours hated him

so much they actually applauded his death, even that
didn't change my mind about Nev. The reason? A
rope trick and the wasp's nest in the backyard.

Mind you, I often wonder why he held my face so
close to the wasp's nest, but on the whole I think
about the rope trick more.

The end.

CATALOGUE

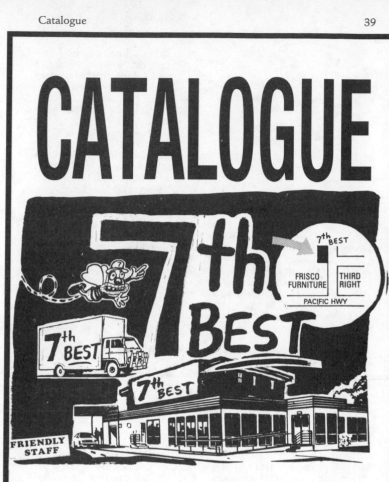

7th Best is an organisation dedicated to creating a world where everyone is equal.

Our scientists and technicians strive to create attention seeking products that will give hope to the unpopular.

Remember, before using any attention seeking products, always look for the 7th Best seal of approval. Otherwise you may be using a superior product and that could lead to over-confidence.

The 7th Best Just Punched COMEDY Sound Samples

Is there anything eternal victims can use to overcome street aggression?

Yes! Our 7th Best *Just punched Comedy Sound Samples* can help.

Say a person is being punched by someone. If the punched person can keep a smile on his or her face or even make the person doing the punching laugh, then they'll be closer to acceptance and hopefully an end to the punching.

By using our 7th Best *Just Punched Comedy Sound Samples* you can retain a sense of humour no matter how much pain you're in.

How does it work?

A person is fitted with over 20 special electronic sound pads. If a fist or a knee or a bike helmet hits you, it touches a pad which inturn triggers a sound sample of something funny.

Imagine the reaction you will get from a stranger punching you and they hear a sample of someone blowing a raspberry or telling a concise but original joke. They start laughing.

The *Just Punched Comedy Sound Samples* turn aggression into comedy.

THE SELF CONSCIOUS SADDLE

Are you self conscious and uncomfortable? I'm quite self conscious but I'm not uncomfortable. In social situations I spend a lot of time sitting on my shoulder trying to look at myself to see myself how others see me and then I act accordingly. I spend more time sitting on my shoulder than I do inside my emotions and that can make me very uncomfortable at times. My technicians at 7th Best have come up with a wonderful new product to give self conscious people, like myself, some dignity or at the very least a straight back. The product is called the *Self Conscious Saddle*—a tiny imaginary saddle that sits on your shoulder and not only adds support but is comfortable. All you do is make an appointment with someone with a 7th Best certificate—virtually everyone's got one, mine's called a HSC—they describe the saddle to you, you imagine it's on your shoulder and that's all there is to it. Being self conscious is one thing but you don't have to be uncomfortable as well. Take the strain out of social pain with a Sandman's Self Conscious Saddle from 7th Best. The end

EMOTIONAL AIR TANKS

Do you find yourself in situations where you don't have the emotional range to cope? Perhaps a friend receives terrible news and all you can say is 'Let go, you're tearing my shirt'.

Then you need the 7th Best *Emotional Air Tanks*.

A quick puff from the emotional tanks, which are easily concealed under any fashionable clothing, and you start acting like a wonderful friend should.

Inside the tanks are stored emotions, exact duplications of emotions belonging to Mother Theresa, Dick Smith and Phoebe Fraser.

We use their spirit of generosity to give you a bigger emotional range. Emotional Air tanks from 7th Best.

We've already had tremendous interest from theatre groups and athletes with media commitments. Please order now before it's too late.

We know the art of compelling is complex.

But we also know that if someone is talking to you and their eyebrows are moving independently of their voice you can be hopelessly intrigued by them.

At 7th Best we don't underestimate eyebrows. We've actually invented our own eyebrows called *Compellors*.

They're activated by a nervous cough and move independently of speech patterns. Even cynical types will be compelled by their dance. In fact they're so lifelike you'll swear something is hatching from them.

Why not be the compelling one yourself. *Compellors*. They look like caterpillars but they act like butterflies.

Available in most hair tones and in paisley for the groovy.

GOSSIPERS

Do you need to have your finger on the pulse in social situations? I know I do.

Why not try *Gossipers*— imaginary wings that allow you to hover emotionally three conversations in front of yourself without anyone knowning.

You'll always be the closest person to the most interesting person in the room because you'll always be the first person to know where the next most interesting person is.

Gossipers are excellent for theatre and gallery openings but they're not out of place at the football either.

We can't make you the most popular person in the room but we guarantee you'll be standing right next to them.

Gossipers require surgery to install but it's only an overnight stay and the scar is covered by hair.

Gossipers from 7th Best

UNDERCOMFORTABLEMENTS

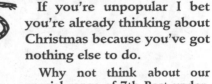

If you're unpopular I bet you're already thinking about Christmas because you've got nothing else to do.

Why not think about our special range of 7th Best undergarments called *Undercomfortablements*?

A piece of string is threaded through a T towel and worn under the pants or a dress.

Undercomfortablements are made to make you look uncomfortable. Even the blandest personalities get a feeling of restlessness which gives the impression of depth; a quality absolutely necessary for people trying to break into an arty crowd.

Make this Xmas the 7th Best time of your life with *Undercomfortablements* from 7th Best

ATTENTION! ATTENTION! WEBBING

Attention! Attention!

Find it hard to keep people interested?

Is your voice a dull throbbing sound to others?

You need *Attention Webbing*. Attention Webbing works just like a spiders web. You know where it is but the web itself is completely invisible to visitors—they get hopelessly stuck. Suddenly you have friends!

'One night I'd invited overseas visitors back to my place. No sooner had Oleg and Stephanie got in the door than they were trapped like small beetles.'

'They didn't even have time to adjust their eyes to the light

before I was showing them my latest Raku fired pinch pots'.

Alleviate the problem of keeping friends interested. Get them tangled up with *Attention Webbing*.

Another 7th Best idea.

Many people come up to me and say 'Sandman, you've got a liver problem. You should see a doctor'.

I have their attention the minute I walk into a room because I'm wearing my 7th Best *Rings of Satan*—specially designed dark liver rings that are fitted and set under the eyes by our technicians at 7th best.

In the 90s we're all looking for an advantage and *Rings of Satan* give you just that.

They snare attention everytime.

The 7th Best *Rings of Satan* are grown from actual skin samples taken from under John English's eyes and they come with the same guarantee for resilience that John has himself.

Look sick for personal gain with 7th Best *Rings of Satan*.

THE MOTORIST'S FRIEND

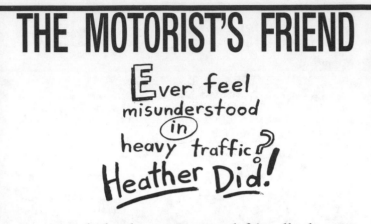

Ever feel misunderstood in heavy traffic? Heather Did!

'I wanted the horn to sound friendly but no matter how delicately I pressed it sounded angry and shrill'.

That's exactly why our technicians at 7th Best designed an emotionally flexible car horn called *The Motorist's Friend*.

If you want to politely let someone in front know the light is green all you do is touch a button, an extendible friendly hand reaches out from your headlight, taps the driver's window and gives him a friendly wave.

The Motorist's Friend personifies your emotional intentions clearly.

JINGLE

I wish their was more courtesy
in our trucks and cars
I wish there was humilty
on our roads and paths.

I scurry across the road
I never impede the flow
and if I see a pidgeon
I stop or swerve or slow.

I am the Motorist's friend.

Surfing Can Cure Your Fear of Shop Assistants

I choose to start the story now.

If you have a fear of shop assistants (like I do), it means you can never buy your own clothes. You have to wait for a birthday or Christmas and hope you get some clothes that fit. That's why I'm eternally stuck in Penguin shirts and tan Bogarts. People think that's what I like because that's what they see me in so that's what they buy me.

When I go up to a shop assistant, I freeze. If they ask me what brand of jeans I'm looking for, I get anxious. On occasions I've been so flustered that I've panicked and said a whisky label instead. 'Could I try on the Glenfiddichs please?'

Here's what to do. Drive to a popular surfing spot and wait. Surfers are often so stoked after a surf they leave their clothes on the roof of their car or just throw their stuff carelessly in the back of a wagon. All you have to do is trail them until their stuff blows off the roof or out the back of their car and it's yours. Last summer I got a pair of board shorts, a leg rope, some eyedrops and a Doberman.

Do be careful to change locations regularly. I was beaten to a pulp behind a boatshed when some locals thought I was with the Federal Police. Nevertheless, I found the beating far less traumatic than buying new clothes from a bubbly shop assistant.

The end.

Double Verbosists

I choose to start the story now.

If each family is a symphony and these symphonies are played together to make society then it must be said my Aunty Coral is the Double Verbose player in our family.

A circular breather is a talkative person. They have the ability to talk and breathe at the same time. Well, now there's a subgroup called the Double Verbosist— a person who has the habit of telling the same person something twice.

A good Double Verbosist, like my Aunty Coral, can disguise a morning spiel with an afternoon one and still be quite interesting. An inferior artist will blindly play the same piece again and again, be it a story about how bandy legs run in the family, or a doctor who has warm hands.

Double Verbosists often live alone, and because silence doesn't talk back, Verbosists sadly lose the ability to listen. They tend to spend their days telling the same story twice to visiting tradespeople.

In a few years we may tell Double Verbose players to shut up, because after the 2000 Olympiad we'll all be rich, but, until then, please watch out for Double Verbose players and their sad sonatas of repetition.

The end.

You Can't Make Mediocre Better

I choose to start the story now.

Our neighbours' son David is three minutes older than me. We were born at the same hospital during a dust storm and it's interesting to see how we've both turned out.

I guess I am what I was expected to be—mediocre. David is mediocre too, but he was expected to be important. According to his parents (both in Retail), he showed all the signs of being a sports champion from a very early age.

At four, David moved tons of sand from one side of his yard to the other in less than a day (using only a toy tip truck). By age 13, his muscles had grown so big he needed to have two shirts joined together to accommodate them.

David played sport, but because he was top heavy and unable to change direction quickly he was not successful. During his twenties he became despondent and his back muscles shifted to the lower part of his body to form a knapsack full of yesterday's muscle.

Last week it was sad to look over the fence and see David climbing to the top of a huge blazing bonfire. Not only because he was badly burned, but because his parents were still egging him on to the top.

I'm glad I was average at sport.

The end.

A Romantic Nickname is a Social Attribute

I choose to start the story now.

My father was a big man but he could creep up behind you without you hearing him because he had the ability to walk lightly.

This trait gave him a certain romantic aura and because of that he was called the 'Man Who Walks Lightly'.

In the first hour of meeting him people's eyes would be fixed on his feet, hoping that the magic of his light walking technique would be revealed. Of course there was nothing magic about his feet at all. My father was just a shy man who laughed at his own jokes. He simply created this expectation by way of his romantic nickname. People really looked forward to meeting him.

Over the past two years I've been visiting people late in the evenings, hoping that I might cultivate the idea of me as someone called 'Sandy Comes Night-time'.

Unfortunately, all the people in my area have young children and go to bed quite early. They get very angry with me when I visit them after midnight.

Nevertheless, don't wait for others to romanticise your life. Do it yourself. Now!

The end.

Inheriting a Parent's Flaws is a Big Weight to Carry

I choose to start the story now.

On school market days most students usually bring something from home to sell. My father said he'd make lemon squash. He had an innate ability to know if someone liked their lemon cordial sweet or watery. He instinctively knew how much cordial to put in a particular person's tumbler just by looking at them. My mother's skill was knowing which ancestor a current family member looked like.

Neither skill was that useful for market day. So in the end my mother decided to make 50 butterfly cakes.

As I suspected, the cakes did not sell. It was as though they had repellent on them and at the end of the day everyone else's tray was empty except mine. It still had

50 cakes on it. So to make our family competitive I
hid behind an oleander bush and ate 25 of them. I
was taught not to waste food.

When I got home my mother thought the cakes
had been such a success that she made them for
every market day after that. By the time I got to high
school I was puffy and bulbous from having eaten
over 350 butterfly cakes in primary school.

Now even if I see the word 'market day' I gain 3
kilos in anticipation of eating butterfly cakes.

The end.

Failure is Hereditary

I choose to start the story now.

Parents usually try and avoid passing the baton of failure to their offspring. My family were no different. There was a period during my late teens when my parents tried very hard to make me look successful.

At the time I was a Fitter's Mate at an industrial complex, but my parents encouraged me to wear a suit to work. It was a quality cloth, tailor made and according to them, something to cherish for the rest of my life.

They also insited I catch the bus to work. Not from the bus stop in front of our house but from the next stop down. (Some 800 metres away.) This was so the neighbours would see me going to work in a suit and think I had an executive job in the city.

Despite needing to sell off some furniture and Mum's wedding pearls, my father backed up our plan to look middle class by buying a late-model Rover with a wooden dashboard.

It wasn't until years later (when I was picking up papers for the Lions Club in Foster and I ran into an old neighbour) that I realised our plan was a dud. She told me everyone in our street used to sarcastically refer to me as the Ordinary Prince in the Special Tan Suit.

Failure is hereditary and unavoidable.

The end.

Make Sure You're Comfortable with Your Habits Before You Turn Twenty

I choose to start the story now.

When you're a teenager choose your habits carefully, because they're hard to change once they're set. For instance, how high do you wear your pants? Are you Harry High or a Larry Low pants? It's important to know. They way you wear your pants says something about you.

I'm a Harry High pants. I simply followed what my father did and he wore his pants high so I did the same. Unfortunately, I take after my mother's side of the family (chunky) and during my early twenties I developed a paunch.

When your pants are up high and you've got a paunch, the material between the crutch and belt area is stretched to the limit. Nowadays I look like I'm wearing an upside-down Pyrex bowl down my pants. Therefore, the pants habit I chose as an impressionable 17 year old doesn't suit me now. Clearly, my body shape is more suited to having the pants pushed low, a bit of cleavage smiling above the belt at the back and my paunch as a feature round the front. This would make me appear warm and natural. Instead, my pants are up high and I look repressed and morose.

Even though it would suit me to have my pants low it doesn't feel right. I wish it did but it doesn't.

It's too late to change anyway.

The end.

Every Street Needs a Tragic Figure

I choose to start the story now.

As I sat on our fence in front of the two poplar trees that obscured my house (if only they were popular trees as I had called them as a child), waiting for my lift to arrive, I was wondering why our family always used to take Mr Fewings (who used to live down the road) with us wherever we went. If we went to the football, we took Mr Fewings. If we went to Lake Conjola for holidays, he'd come to. All we got in return for our efforts were blackfish. If blackfish had been the local currency, we'd have been rich with the amount of fish Mr Fewings gave us.

The sound of a car horn broke my reflection. It was the Bolands. They were honking because I was going to look for golf balls with them.

As I shut their car door and returned the window to the closed position, to save my hair from losing its wave, it suddenly occurred to me why we used to take Mr Fewings with us. Every generation in every street has to have a Mr Fewings to feel sorry for. It makes your own life seem a little less tragic when

you know there is someone worse off than you
around.

As we drove to the driving range I suspected I
might be the Mr Fewings figure in the Bolands' lives.
The only difference was that I gave the Bolands golf
balls instead of blackfish. I felt different about the
Boland family after that day.

The end.

The Morose Teenager Technique

I choose to start the story now.

After a few moselles does your Aunty Coral start telling stories about magpies with human characteristics and you can't break into the conversation because she's mastered the art of circular breathing conversation?

Do you have a relative who turns up with presents for everyone but no one ever has anything for him/her, so you secretly wrap a bottle of cherries in brandy, which is the actual present he/she gave you last Xmas?

It needn't be like this. Not with The Sandman's Morose Teenage Technique—based on the principle you don't have to impress relatives. You can be as morose as you like and not suffer any consequences socially.

When you enter a relative's home, just let one thing bug you. Perhaps your Uncle Bill makes an irritating sound when he eats? A 'mm mm' type of sound. If you keep focusing on that one thing, I guarantee it will turn you into the morose 17 year old you once were. You'll be difficult, uncooperative and completely left alone.

Warning. To ensure ongoing affection from your family do be nice during the last 10 minutes of your visit.

The end.

When You Squeeze Something Too Tightly, Sometimes You Can't Tell What It Is

I choose to start the story now.

People with an overdeveloped sense of loss tend to hold on to things so tightly they forget what they're actually holding on to.

I hated seeing my father go to work. Even as a teenager I'd still chase his car down the street yelling, 'Dad! Dad! Please come back.' At times I was so emotional I didn't realise I was chasing the neighbour's car. Dad apparently used to slip out the back and ride his bike to work. I was holding on to my past so tightly I couldn't recognise it any more.

My uncle Nev (before he was killed) said you can judge a person by the firmness of their handshake. He squeezed a hand so violently he couldn't possibly judge anything about anyone. He was so intense when he shook your hand that all the capillaries on his face would rise to the surface like a replica of the Menindee lake system. Yet he still had the gall to tell you what was wrong with you according to your handshake! Every hand he shook must have felt like a squashed banana. I once placed a tack in between my index finger and second finger but even that failed to make an impression on Uncle Nev. He just kept on squeezing.

Don't hold on too tightly. Nobody wants their past to be a squashed banana.

The end.

Most People Inherit a Family Trait

I choose to start the story now.

Perhaps your mother is double-jointed and showed promise at jazz ballet, and you've often wondered why you can move creatively to the sound of James Morrison but not Tommy Emmanuel?

That was Lucky...

Or perhaps your father had high insteps and could beat a racehorse over 25 metres and you too can beat most animals off the mark in a sprint race?

These are family traits. Heirlooms from an ancestral gene pool, passed on to give you something in life to build on.

It took me a long time to find out what trait I'd inherited. In fact, it took a chance conversation with Aunty Coral—she can read and listen at the same time—to discover my father was good at avoiding rabbits while driving a car. He had the ability to see a rabbit before others plus the skill to swerve his car and miss it.

Since that time, I've been driving around western New South Wales hoping a rabbit would appear so I could miss it. Obviously the trait is rabbit specific, because I clipped a chap on a pushbike in Junee. If it'd been a rabbit on a bike, I bet I would have missed him.

The end.

Eat with an Older Person– It Can Make You Younger

I choose to start the story now.

When you're young you have plenty of time left so you tend to leave everything to the last minute. When you get older, you tend to get ready for things earlier in order to save time. You start packing your bags two weeks before a holiday starts, waiting for a cab the second after you've booked it, or you start thinking about next Christmas on Boxing Day.

Perhaps you've noticed when you visit your older relatives, you just finish chewing your lunch and suddenly it's dinnertime once more? There doesn't appear to be an afternoon period.

Visiting my Aunty Coral is like going back in time. Her house full of Nanna things, there's a faint smell of mould which teases the most resilient of nostrils and she starts preparing dinner so early it's actually lunch. That's a saving of five hours.

Therefore if I go to my Aunty Coral's for dinner it's possible for me to gain five hours of life. If I was to eat dinner at Aunty Coral's twice a week for 16 years, I'd be one year younger.

I might be 20 kilos heavier because Aunty Coral likes fried food, but I certainly would be younger.

My Aunty Coral is a time machine.

The end.

Waiting is a Hobby for People with No Other Interests

I choose to start the story now.

As a rule I'm not good at 'activities' but I am good at waiting. I'm relaxed at red lights. I'm happy waiting in a line to buy tickets and I'm excellent at waiting for much anticipated mail to arrive. I'm never agitated by slow service at a cafe (in fact, I find it amusing). I'm good at waiting for something to happen, too. I just wait for an extroverted person to start something off then I latch on. Rather like a pilot fish does. I never cried while I was waiting to see Santa. I cried when I got on his lap but never in the line, and I was always good at being the reserve— patient and quiet. Coaches often took the time to mention it to my parents.

I think my love of waiting was formed many years ago, while I was waiting to see if my father would be home before his dinner got too dry to eat. Even if I was sick I wouldn't go to sleep until I heard his handbrake in the carport and smelt his dry shepherd's pie being eaten. Or at least the sound of it getting scraped off a plate and the flip-top bin closing.

I wholeheartedly recommend waiting. You can do it all your life and it's something you can do when you're lonely.

The end.

Talk, Touch and Take Technique

I choose to start the story now.

I only ever visit untidy friends because they always have boxes, books and ornamnets lining their hallways. These are potential cheap presents and here's how to get them.

The next time you arrive at an untidy friend's house, walk slowly down their hallway and make a mental not of what's there and what you want.

When it's time to leave, place yourself in fornt of the host so that when you get to the item you've selected, let's say a raku-fired pinchpot, you can stop, touch the item lightly and say, 'That looks nice.'

Remember, you only get one chance or you look pushy.

Nine times out of ten, the host will say to you, 'Oh, you like that? Take it!'

Talk, Touch and Take. It really works.

Be careful though. Untidy people often have dim hallways, it can be hard to see your prey properly. I once visitied an untidy friend and made a note of what I thought was Captain Sinbad book. I couldn't stop thinking about it over lunch. I applied my Talk Touch Take Technique to a tee, but it was so damn dark in that hallway I panicked. When I got outside I found the book I snared was *Send the Stumps Flying, The Science of Fast Bowling*—which I already had.

My visit was completely wasted.

The end.

Sandman's Recipe for a Successful Party

I choose to start the story now.

First you need heat beads—old friends who know most of the people you've invited. Heat beads arrive early, stay in the same spot, hold a lot of grog, never spew, are good listeners and can drive home no matter how drunk they are.

Next are the Hummingbirds. Folks who do lots of arm flapping but have very little forward movement. Hummingbirds arrive at 10 pm, suck lots of nectar and use the same shallow story in different parts of the room. Their vigorous wing flapping fans your all-important heat beads so they're primed for the arrival of your ace party card—the Metho.

Metho are the type of people who ignite every party. They arrive at midnight drunk, turn up the music, light a fart, dance into a wall, vomit and leave. All within the space of an hour. Like a worker bee, their life span is short but essential to the success of any party.

Sometimes they're accompanied but a Pilot Fish—a less compelling person who attaches themselves to a more exciting person for personal gain (a bit like the National Party).

Finally, you add the Sand to put out the fire. Sand is someone who doesn't know anyone. They're told it's a fancy dress party that starts late so they turn up as a tube of toothpast at 1.30 am. I guarantee people will leave within 20 minutes.

Throw a Sandman party. You won't regret it.

The end.

Know a Place Where You Can Get Touched, Laughed At and Made to Feel Superior for $136

I choose to start the story now.

Recently I rode in an ambulance and it's one of the best things I've ever done. The good times started immediately the ambulance arrived and one of the officers took my pulse. It was my first physical contact with a human in three years. Beats brushing up against people at the shops.

Even though my symptoms disappeared after I breathed into a paper bag, I decided to take up their offer to go in the ambulance. It was only $136 and I had nothing better on.

As we drove towards the hospital, one of the officers listened to everything I said. I've never held anyone's interest for 8 kilometres before. For insurnace though, I made sure my toe without the toenail was visible so we could discuss that if we got stuck for conversation.

It was the final part of the experience (at casualty) that was the most rewarding. I'll never forget being put on a trolley and getting pushed past a long line of injured and bleeding people who were waiting for treatment. I can still see the envy in their eyes.

I'll also never forget when one of the officers leaned over and whispered 'It's always crowded on Fridays.' I said, 'It must be spleen night.'

I remember it vividly because the officer laughed at me. I was touched, laughed at and made to feel superior for just $136.

The end.

Be Prepared for Unexpected Social Situations

I choose to start the story now.

Since experiencing an earthquake in Wollongong during the eary '70s, I always wear a nice outfit to bed.

It was about 5.30 am when the earthquake struck. Aunty Coral had just woken me up to give me a port eggflip when suddenly things were flying everywhere. In a panic we both ran out onto the road to see our neighbours, compare damages and help catch their frightened pets.

It took me five minutes to realise I was actually naked from the waist down. Mr Gumley, the next-door neighbour, was even more exposed. He was dressed in a leather lap-lap, moccasins and what appeared to be a gasoline-powered skivvy.

After that incident I was never allowed into the Gumley's house for Milo again. In fact, that street was never the same after the earthquake.

Recently I was in another town when they experienced an earth tremor. That particular night I'd slept in a pair of Jag jeans, Roman sandals and a bone-coloured shirt. The only thing I had to do before racing outside was put water on my hair to reduce the bouffant effect I got from sleeping with a wet head.

I was socially composed when I ran onto the street that day. Everyone said do.

The end.

How to Beat the Popularity Equation

I choose to start the story now.

If you surf and you'r not a very good surfer, chances are you're a very unpopular surfer. Perhaps you've got a long torso and short legs which causes you to nosedive? Whatever the reason, the equation is the same. Expertise = respect = popularity. I'm a poor surfer myself, but here's how I beat the equation.

At East Beach, south of Kiama, 15 foot lefts were peeling off the northern headland. Clingwrap, Brainiac, Tonk and myself decided to go out. I'd much rather have sat in the car, but peer pressure being what it is, I pretended otherwise. I knew the moment the sets came they'd tease me for not taking off and I'd cry.

One by one the others took off on a green

monster, forming a club for those who'd caught a wave. After 15 minutes I was the only one not in the club. So to avoid the embarrassment I paddled north around the headland and kept going until I reached Kiama boat harbour about 9.00 that night.

When we met later that evening, everyone thought I'd actually gone right on a 15 foot left hander. They were so in awe of me and my legendary feat they changed my nickname from Punching Bag to Crazy Cock. Now I always go the opposite way to the break. I fall off at the bottom of every wave but no one can judge whether or not I can surf.

To enhance my 'maddie' image I also surf in pantihose and a lumber jacket. Even though I'm inadequate, I'm a legend.

The end.

The Sure-fire Test for True Friendship

I choose to start the story now.

How do you know what a friend really thinks of you? Do they prove their love when they comfort you in a time of need. Or when they apply a sour-smelling balm to an infected sea ulcer on your foot? Well I've developed a simple friendship test that is both accurate and fun to do.

When your so-called friend is in the shower, just creep into their bedroom and put a threatening mask on your face. When your friend comes back to their room and switches on the light, you simply jump out and say in a very loud voice, 'Hello there.'

The results are quick, simple and accurate. If they're still friendly towards you after the incredible shock passes, they're a true friend. If they're angry then they're not. If they die from fright, that's one less Xmas present to worry about.

Two important things to look out for when using the Sure-fire Friendship Test. Be sure you've got the right house and make sure your so-called friend is not doing something in the shower that takes a long while.

If you're alone in someone's dark bedroom (wearing a threatening mask) for over 10 minutes, you do begin to feel very weird.

The end.

When Your Host is a Dog Lover

I choose to start the story now.

When I went to a stranger's house for a party their dog Nolan barked at every guest except me. Nolan is one of those dogs that barks at everything (pegs, leaves), so when he didn't bark at me that gave me a headstart socially. I actually gave the hosts a fright because no one heard me come in to the party. One of the hosts even said 'That's odd. Usually Nolan barks at strangers.'

After that, whenever new guests arrived, the host would point to me and say, 'Guess what? Nolan didn't bark at him. Whoever he is.'

I was instantly special while the party was young and awkward and people were still tentative and sober.

If you know in advance your hosts are dog lovers, just step in two piles of hamburger mince before you go out. Dogs follow you while the odour lasts and the host will remember you because their dog appears to love you.

Nobody need ever know about your little trick either. Not unless they drop their keys and smell the mince as they bend down to pick them up.

Having the host's dog love you has other advantages. It helps you look occupied when no one else is talking to you and chatting with a dog gives you a chance to eavesdrop. You don't have to listen to a dog, so your ears are free to pick up on other things.

The end.

Beware of the Prairie Dog Syndrome

I choose to start the story now.

Prairie Dogs always appear as if they're spying on someone. In other words, they're curious neighbours. The Prairie Dog Syndrome occurs when a person tries to interpret their neighbour's smells and noises. It's a condition prevalent in buildings where people live closely as strangers.

It may start with a resident analysing the cooking smells coming from an upstairs apartment. 'Mmm, steak with garlic. He's entertaining his Ukrainian friend again.'

This sounds harmless enough, but eventually a Prairie Dog needs to confirm what they smell and this is when the condition gets dangerous. They become so addicted to thier neighbour's social life that they're willing to risk their own life to find out what's going on in their neighbour's apartment.

If you live upstairs and a little bubble of hair is bobbing up and down over your railing, it's fair to assume your downstairs neighbour has Prairie Dog Syndrome. It's bad enough that someone is monitoring your smells, but it's downright disturbing if you live on the tenth floor and someone is dangling from your verandah every other day.

To stop Prairie Dog Syndrome occurring just tie cushions to the bottom of your feet, don't flush the toilet and eat out.

Of course you run the risk of sounding and smelling boring.

The end.

Find Your True Voice in a Car

I choose to start the story now.

Trying to find youself can be a humiliating, expensive and time-consuming experience. Don't despair. There is a place where you can find your true voice that's convenient, private, and in some cases, already paid for—your car.

Inside a car people often reveal themselves emotionally. Folk who you thought were meek may turn out to be Mussolini. Cold fish can suddenly turn flirtatious. Even selfish people may display a huge desire to be loved, continually letting other drivers into a line of traffic just to get a nod of approval.

I discovered my true voice in my Gemini. I was stopped at some traffic lights in Adelaide when a family pulled up next to me and appeared to find me amusing for some reason. Without hesitation, I took my shoes and socks off, wound down the passenger window, slipped the socks onto my hands to make two puppets and put on a brief improvised show with a moral.

When the lights changed the family moved off all smiles. I was abused by the driver behind because he had to wait while I put my shoes and socks back on.

That day in Adelaide I discovered I was a showoff who irritated people. The driver behind me discovered he didn't suffer fools gladly. The smiling family found out they were easily pleased.

The end.

Bold Actions Create Opportunites for Others

I choose to start the story now.

One summer a surfer from my beach called Melon joined the army, but after one week of service he changed his mind and went AWOL. To everyone's surprise Melon turned up at the beach in drawn-on side levers, hoping that his disguise would help him avoid the Military Police.

Luckily, on the day the police did turn up, the sand was hot and it made Melon's knees spring up high which gave him an extra yard of pace. He reached the water's edge well in front of the MPs. I was emerging from the surf, having just spent a frustrating hour in the white water. Without a word Melon grabbed my surfboard and paddled it out the back, leaving the woollen-suited MPs stranded at the high tidemark.

For four days Melon paddled around the breakers. During the daytime he found refuge in the overcrowded take-off area and at night he hid in a nearby breakwater.

That summer was good for everyone. The kiosk devised a waterproof meal (they later sold it to the navy), which the boat crew would secretly drop off while they were training. A local surf shop got free advertising on the TV news when they gave Melon a wetsuit with their logo on it, and because Melon had my board, it gave me a solid connection with the hot surfers who sat near the Norfolk pines.

It was the best summer of my life.

The end.

Extra Chilli Means You Don't Have to Share

I choose to start the story now.

When you have little in life you tend to hog what little you have and this leads to trouble with sharing.

I have very little in life that is uniquely mine. The clothes I buy are the ones I see on other people, the decorations I have in my flat are conepts I've stolen from happy attractive couples, the ideas I believe in and sometimes heatedly defend are borrowed from others. The only thing that is truly mine is my food, and for that reason I find it very hard to share it with anyone.

To overcome this unappealing habit I put an excessive amount of chilli on all my food. I can offer a portion of whatever it is I have to anyone because when a person sees the fine layer of chilli powder on my food they usually decline my offer. Extra chilli means you appear generous even though you're not.

Also, if a person does take a bite you then have the satisfaction of watching them suffer chilli afterburn. (I love that.)

It takes a while to adjust to chilli on cake and in beverages like tea, but it can be done. The only real side effect is a burning ring of fire after your first ablution. If you keep the windows closed, the screams don't attract too much attention.

The end.

The Sandman Songbook

Better With His Hands.

Sit-ting on a towel with you in a pad-dock a hawk up a-bove it
seems so ro-man-tic I let my hand —, brush your arm the
lust in my bo-dy gives me quite a charm This was the mo-ment I
should-'ve said 'I love you' I felt that you felt the same
Let's tell the truth there's no-thing in our way 'cept this hawk buzzin round a-bout a
mile a-way then I close my eyes and kiss you you move a bit and I
miss you oh I re-coil a lit-tle I try not to pan-ic
no sud-den move-ments no-thing dram-a-tic I can't let you know you
hurt my pride and I'm a-good at keep-in things locked in side
May-be you've just got pins and nee-dles in your toes or you don't like the air
com-in from my nose, oh let's tell the truth there's no-thing in our way, cept this

A Man Who's Better With his Hands

Sitting on a towel with you in a paddock.
A hawk up above, it seems so romantic.
I let my hand brush your arm,
the lust in my body gives me quite a charm

This is the moment I want to say I love you.
I feel that you feel the same.
Let's tell the truth, there's nothing in our
way.
'Cept this hawk buzzin round about a mile
away.

Then I close my eyes and kiss you.
You move a bit and I miss you. Oh.

I recoil a little, I try not to panic.
No sudden movements, nothing dramatic.
I can't let, you know you hurt my pride,
and I'm good at keeping things locked inside.

Maybe you've just got pins and needles in
your toes.
Or you don't like the air comin' from my
nose.
Let's tell the truth, there's nothing in our
way.

'Cept this hawk buzzing round about a mile away.

Then I close my eyes and kiss you.
You move a bit and I miss you. Oh.

Then you say you'd rather, have a man,
who is better with his hands.

If it is sex, please put me to the test,
I was taught by an older woman, how to do my best.
Let's tell the truth, there's nothing in our way.
'Cept this hawk buzzin round about a mile away.

Repeat chorus.

I Felt Important (I was overconfident)

I felt important when I picked the restaurant.
And I felt important 'cos I knew the menu I
could tell you what to order.
I felt important when we talked of marriage.
And I felt important on couple's nights,
when we were the couple who would never
fight.
And I felt important on Saturdays.
'Cos boys' night out was Fridays.

But I nearly died when you broke it off.

I felt important 'cos your big brother was a
very hot surfer.
And I felt important when I saw the suntan
mark from the ring I bought ya.
And on the physical hierarchy,
you were much more attractive than me.

But I nearly died, when I read it on a bench,
you were dating someone else, then I read it
on a fence as well.

I was overconfident.
There was too much me.
I was overconfident.
I should change.

Nicole

Nicole

Thought that I'd be married at least,
by the time I was twenty three.
Or that I might be engaged.
In my mind it was arranged.

Virginia and I talked family.
Designed the kids we'd like to see.
Hair and nose from her side of things,
eyes and skin designed by me.

It took six weeks for us to build it,
just one hour to turn sour.

Then I met Nicole.
Then I met Nicole.
Then I met Nicole.
And she blew me out.

Is She
~~I Think My Mum's~~ Attracted To That Guy.

page 1.

I re-call a hos-pit-al a guy in my ward fond my Mum at-tract-ive.

He'd des-cribe her nak-ed al-ways caught him watch-ing her

un-der-neath his blank-et. Vis-it-ing twice a day

and beds close e-nough for them to be ac-quaint-ed

Flash-ing eyes looks ex-changed I think that Mum re-cip-ro-cat-ed

Does she have af-fairs___? Does she fan-ta-si-i-i-i-ise?

Is she at-tract-ed to this guy?

I hoped his wound in-fect-ed so his stay in hos-pit-al

might be ex-tend-ed. 'cos it's strange to share an ail-ment with a

guy who wants your Mum for ro-man-tic in-volve-ment

But o-ver time I'd have to say ev-en though I tried

not to I found him O.K. Should I tell Dad a-bout it?

Is She Attracted to That Guy?

I recall, a hospital.
A guy in my ward found my mum attractive.

He'd describe, her naked,
always found him watching her from
underneath his blanket.

Visiting, was twice a day, beds close,
enough for them to be acquainted.

Flashing eyes, looks exchanged.
I think that Mum reciprocated.

Does she have affairs?
Does she fantasise?
Is she attracted to that guy?

At first, I hoped his wound infected,
so his stay in hospital, might be extended.

But over time, I'd have to say,
even though I tried to, I found him okay.

So should I tell Dad about it?
That would spoil Mum's fun, no doubt about
it.

Does she have affairs?
Does she fantasise?
Is she attracted to that guy?
Is Mum attacted to that guy?
I think she's attracted to that guy?

You Get Strength from Failed Relationships

I choose to start the story now.

I've had only one long-term relationship in my life. Six weeks by the sea with my beloved Virginia that ended when I made it quite clear I didn't want to have sex seven times a week.

Virginia usually went to bed first. She was often tired from her day job as a Rugby League referee. I was doing my HSC at TAFE for the fifth time so I didn't have to be up until early October. I'd wait till I thought she was asleep then I'd creep into the bedroom. As a precaution I'd put luminous tape on all the creaky floorboards. The slightest noise would awaken a desire in her that I could never seem to satisfy.

Once at the bed I'd lower myself slowly onto the mattress. However, even if I slept on the side of the bed, a section no wider than the width of a slice of devon, I knew her fingers would eventually find my back and walk down across my stomach.

During those six weeks I built up immense upper body strength and developed calf muscles with a lovely almond shape from lowering myself slowly onto the bed.

I gained strength from my failed romance.

The end.

Stand Somewhere You've Never Stood Before

I choose to start the story now.

There's a lot of things an awkward person may never do. An awkward person may never play sport for Australia, make someone weep with joy by preparing a celestial meal, or even have a relationship that lasts more than six weeks. But there's no reason for an awkward person to feel stagnant.

No matter how unpopular you are there's one thing you can do and you don't have to leave the house to do it. Simply stand in the parts of your house that you've never stood in before.

I was feeling stagnant after failing everything in my HSC when I realised I'd never stood in the gap between the bookcase and the right-hand wall in my loungeroom. I looked at it every day but I'd never stood there. With the help of a friend, I moved the bookcase away from the wall and stood in the gap, and to be honest, I felt quite strong standing there. My visitor even thought I looked handsome in the golden light that was coming through a small dirty window on the other side of the room.

I found doing this was better than doing nothing and I'd been somewhere I'd never been before.

It was also good having another perspective on my loungeroom, too.

The end.

If You Cling to One Thing for Too Long You Become Unusual and Hard to Know

I choose to start the story now.

Ken Sorenson (along with myself) was an eternal reserve for junior Rugby League teams. Many times we shared the sideline and talked about our dream of playing representative Rugby League. My involvement in the game had faded but Ken is an 'emotional gecko'. Sticky pads on his personality allow him to cling onto impossible situations.

When I went home, I made it my business to see Ken. He still had my sheet music to 'Crocodile Rock' and I wanted it back. Sure enough he was at the football, still a reserve for a local 3rd-grade team. I sat down next to him and gently said, 'Ken,'

After a long pause he looked up at me and said, 'If I get a run today, I'll head-butt him staightaway, in the first scrum. I'll head-butt him some and I'll be in the team next week.'

Ken
Sorenson

My smile must have looked like somebody was operating my lips with fishing line from behind my back.

He continued. 'I'll tell him his mother's a druggie, he'll stick up his head like a goose, and in the first scrum, I'll head-butt him some, and I'll be in the team next week.'

I got up slowly and moved away until I thought I was out of sight. Then I ran.

Two things disturbed me in the three minutes I'd spent with Ken. He seemed very angry and he talked exclusively in rhyming couplets. In my opinion, Ken hung onto his dream for too long and now he was unusual and hard to know.

The end.

Sandman's Advice To The Unpopular

Just Because it's Not Used Doesn't Mean it's Not Needed

I choose to start the story now.

Recently I went out 'on the town'. I hadn't been on the town for six years (I'm afraid of bourbon), and I don't know if it was me, the weather, or what, but at every club somebody tried to take my self-esteem away. It was as if it was a luxury item and fair game. Admittedly I never use my self-esteem, but that doesn't mean I won't need it one day.

It was like when Paul Vanderbelt convinced me that his family never used their downstairs shower. So we cut a piece of pipe out of it to use as a steering column in our go-cart.

It was the first time I'd ever been hit by someone else's parent. Mr Vanderbelt's words are still vivid to me. Each one coughed out after every blow of his belt. 'Just-because-it's-not-used-doesn't-mean-it's-not-needed-San-dy.' Keep in mind I was twenty at the time.

If you attend nightclubs and you see someone whose lips are thin, torso is pear-shaped, wearing a lemon Penguin shirt and tan Bogarts, it's possibly me. And I'd like to keep my self-esteem for the future.

The end.

Sandman's Snowy Story and a Bent Passenger Door

I choose to start the story now.

In some social scenes it's hard to make your mark until you've done something legendary. If you have a fear of danger/embarrassment but you would like to make a mark in your social scene, then try my Legendary Snowy Story and a Bent Passenger Door.

Firstly, and very importantly, bend the passenger door of your car downwards so it doesn't shut properly. If you're not prepared to do that then stop reading now.

This is so the next time the boys pile into your car, to go to the place where unattractive males go after the pub closes and the guy sitting in your passenger seat says, 'Your door doesn't shut mate', you can say 'Going down to the Snowy I hung my arse out the door and scraped it on the bitumen at 120 k. It bent the door.'

It's the last time you'll be considered unremarkable by your peers. You don't have to eat a seagull, hop out of a moving vehicle or head-butt a beer can to impress anyone either. You just bend the passenger door of your car so it's consistent with my Snowy Story and you have all the credibility you need.

Things will turn around for you. I promise.

The end.

How to Get Back at Someone if You're Shy

I choose to start the story now.

There's only the one entertainment facility where I go for my annual holidays—a small open-air cinema that's been run by the same man for years.

Normally his volunteer cinematic efforts are much loved. This one particular year (when he was quite ill), he was harshly criticised for letting the standard of his facility drop.

The manager is a shy, eager to please, keen-not-to-make-a-fuss type of person. He is not the sort who shows his anger publicly. So in order to get revenge on his critics (in a way that suited him) he started presenting perverse double features, ie *Bedroom Mazurka* and *Flipper and the Pirates*.

Campers still loved the shy manager and his eccentric habits but his odd combinations of films did leave a sour taste in the mouths of most holiday-makers that year. Especially the parents who sat through *Bedroom Mazurka* with their kids so they could see *Flipper and the Pirates* afterwards.

If you're meek and you need to retaliate, try perversity. It works! It's non-violent, juvenile and there's a sense of fun that ensures you remain loved.

Perversity keeps you young.

The end.

The Billet—A Middle-class Dilemma

I choose to start the story now.

Standing with your team-mates in a strange city waiting to be introduced to a billet typifies the middle-class dilemma. On the one hand you're excited to have escaped from your parents. On the other hand you wish they were there to help you deal with the strange surroundings.

There's the drive to a billet's house in an odd-smelling car. The teenage daughter who doesn't hide her disappointment that it's you who's the billet and not Danny Conner, who has shoulder-length blond hair and piercing blue eyes.

There's the 45-minute hay fever attack in a musty bedroom. The rope ladder you need to get out of bed because the sag in the mattress is so deep it's more like a ravine than a bed. A shower so furious that the water cuts your skin. Shampoo that gives your hair so much body it's like having a helium balloon on top of your head. The toilet paper that chafes so severely you can sharpen pencils in your bottom, and of course, the eyes of the family that follow you silently throughout your dinner rituals.

Morning. Time to join your team-mates in town. As you climb into the car you wish you could have spent the night unattended at the Police Boys Club like some of the rougher guys did. Then again, you also wish your parents would turn up with some roast chicken and cold potatoes.

The end.

Evolution

I choose to start the story now.

I was sitting with my dog, 'The Tight Piece of Work', watching him look at two dogs that were playing in the park. I couldn't let him out because other dogs beat him up. At any rate, he seemed satisfied perched up on a pot plant, standing on his hind legs, looking over the balcony.

I thought, isn't it sad that nature only allows him to hold the two-legged position in short bursts. It then occurred to me that if I was to keep Tight inside all his life then he might develop huge leg muscles. One day he may be able to walk permanently on his hind legs. Or at least his descendants may evolve into a species of walking dog.

If this is true then my neighbour, who has the habit of spying over the top of her high wooden fence, may find that her descendants' eyes will be closer to their hairlines and they won't have to stand on their tippy toes to spy on their neighbours anymore. Perhaps they'll develop explosive calf muscles and be good hurdlers.

In my own family (a vulnerable and insecure people), perhaps constant repression may cause our future generations to develop impregnable defense mechanisms to protect them from witty people.

Just then Tight toppled off the

balcony—a fall of about 5 metres. As I looked for an after-hours vet I realised my theory had a way to go yet.

The end.

Failure Requires No Preparation

I choose to start the story now.

When I came first in the handwriting contest, I got to write to our school's pen friend in Hong Kong. Sadly, my success was a major chore as it meant I had to sit in a room during lunch hours and write out letters on behalf of the school.

Not only was I missing out on lunch, I was missing opportunities to impress others in the playground. It was also disturbing to see the contents of my school bag shoot past the window so often.

Each letter took longer to write than I would have liked because my actual winning handwriting sample was done by my mother. She did all my homework—be it Maths or building a Pinocchio ring game from plywood for Craft.

In a way, I was responsible for my mother being educated twice. Not many women of her generation can say that.

Sitting alone in that room also made me realise that success requires sacrifice, whereas failure is preparation free. If I'd have submitted my own work I might have failed, but I would have been out in the playground trying to impress others.

I was a success stuck in an empty room.

The end.

Sometimes it's Best Not to Know

I choose to start the story now.

The summer I met Virginia we visited her parents' hobby farm and stayed in their shed. I was happy because only couples stayed in the shed. The singles had to go to the caravan park. Very severe if you were part of the scene but single.

During that visit I helped Virginia's father lay a concrete slab. I've never been good with my hands so it was exhilarating to use all the different tools that can spread cement.

When I went the second time, I knew Alan (Virginia's 'touchy feely' friend) would be there. They were often together, holding hands, giggling and generally being on the same wavelength. Therefore Alan and I would be in direct competition for a couples' berth.

When I arrived, Virginia was waiting at the gate. I stopped the Gemini and signalled for her to open it so I could drive up the track and honk the horn like other visitors did. Instead of opening the gate Virginia said I had to go with Brainiac, Two Dicks and Trudy to the caravan park.

'But we're a couple, I deserve to be in the shed.'

'That's not the issue,' she replied.

'Oh! What is? Alan?'

'No, my father hates you.'

I was restless at the caravan park. Not only because Two Dicks was a pyromaniac but because I'd never known what was built on the concrete slab.

At least it adds mystery to an otherwise flat life.

The end.

It's Important that the Time You Spend at Home is the High Point of Your Life

I choose to start the story now.

Spending time at my house can be quite flat. Nevertheless, with a bit of pre-planning I can trick myself into thinking otherwise.

For example, I make sure the road I take to get to my house is quite demanding. That way I have to concentrate on my driving rather than think about how much I'd like to be going to someone else's place. I also drive past the nicer homes in my area so I think I live in a well-to-do suburb, and when I leave my house I always take the busiest road. If the traffic is particularly bad then I can't wait to get back home again.

You may find it's hard to keep tricking yourself. There may even be periods when your house is less than interesting, so set challenges for yourself.

Instead of using the front door to enter your house,

crawl in through a small window that's quite high up
so it's a relief to get in the house. If you're thirsty,
park a couple of blocks away so you can't wait to get
inside and have a cordial. Or when you go off to
work, leave your pants behind. That way you'll
always be in a hurry to get back home and put them
on again.

If you make the world around you seem bleak, the
time spent in your house will be like a paradise.

The end.

When You're Self-obsessed, Stand Next to a Good Listener

I choose to start the story now.

I'm self-obsessed and I find it hard to understand anything I don't say or write. I'm often lost and bewildered by pamphlets and other people's conversations.

At school I only ever read the first two lines of any exam paper. If my name wasn't mentioned, I'd lose interest immediately. What worked the third time I repeated Year 12 was writing an exam paper in my own handwriting. This tactic made me more inclined to succeed. Unfortunately, by the time I'd written out the exam paper there was no time to do the actual exam. Still, I understood the questions more thoroughly than the previous three times I'd sat the HSC.

I have the same problem with conversations. When someone talks to me, I turn off unless the subject matter relates to me. To combat this I stand next to people who appear to understand what's being said and do whatever they do.

It's the same when I read a traffic sign. I wait till someone else reads it then I follow them.

It's frustrating being lost for much of your life but at least I don't have to think of others.

The end.

A Fear of Shop Assistants Almost Made Me Turn to Crime

I choose to start the story now.

When Nick the Dip approached me at the hotel and said 'Come out to my car Sandy, I've got a proposition for you', I was worried.

I was sure he'd found out I'd stolen bricks from a building site he controlled. Or he was still angry about me being indirectly responsible for the death of his two greyhounds when the rifle range fell down on top of them.

There were two other people inside the car. Norman—who'd once run through a plate of glass window in a bike helmet for a bet—and Nick's girlfriend Louise, who was reading a copy of *American Psycho*.

After a short but very disturbing pause, Nick said, 'Sandy, how would you like to drive a car in a robbery? We're going to knock over a clothes shop. There's $100 plus a couple of pairs of jeans in it for you.'

I certainly didn't need the money—I'm middle class—but the possibility of picking up a couple of pairs of jeans without having to face a bubbly shop assistant was enticing. If I took part in the robbery, I would not have to go into a jean shop for a couple of years.

Sadly, the stress of being a criminal lowered my defences. I got glandular fever and was unable to take part in the robbery.

I guess it's another year of wearing tan Bogarts.

The end.

Even in Dreams I Seem to Fail

I choose to start the story now.

I recently dreamt I was in the back of an independent bands truck with Madonna and she was very attracted to me. We started kissing. Her lips were swollen and her tongue was confident as it patrolled the inside of my mouth. It was good. Very good.

Not knowing what to do next, I tried to say 'I've only got one filling. My saliva is very strong.' But before I could finish the sentence she lay her index finger across my lips, which made the words after 'saliva' sound like 'swilwing'.

She loosened my belt. It was the first time anyone but me had ever done that. I desperately wanted to

do something for her just in case I disappointed her within the next minute, but she insisted I lie still so she could run her fingers around the rim of my nostrils (the need to sneeze only adding to the tension). If I was a stuffed camel I would have torn apart the wool stitches that held me together.

Then suddenly my wonderful sexy dream was interrupted by a stupid recurring dream I've had since childhood. I'm the captain of a big navy ship and none of the crew has slept for 70 hours so we pull into a fiord to rest and make minor repairs.

It was a very disappointing end to the dream. I was cranky after that.

The end.

The No-one Ever Comes Back from Goodbye Technique

I choose to start the story now.

I've discovered a way for insignificant people to be compelling. It's called the No-one Comes Back from Goodbye Technique and I came across it while visiting an elderly relative of mine.

In the past, when I visited this particular elderly relative and I was nice to her, she'd press $20 into my hand. On the day in question, I'd displayed bad manners and she didn't give me any money. So when I got on the bus I was very depressed.

However, my mood changed the moment I walked down the aisle of the bus. All the other passengers were staring at me, looking out the back window to where my elderly relative was standing and then looking back at me. Some were even waving to my relative. I'm sure they felt this would be the last time we'd be saying goodbye to each other because she looked so close to death and I appeared so down.

Now I visit her every weekend. We've even worked on the act. I bought her an aqua cardigan so she'd stand out more and she had the idea of not moving until the bus was completely out of sight. Watching her become a tiny aqua speck through the back window of the bus really enhances the feeling of loss.

Now, every Sunday, without fail, my elderly relative and I emotionally affect the passengers travelling on the 391 to the city.

The end.

If Something's on Your Mind, Say it Sooner Rather than Later

I choose to start the story now.

On a trip to Gosford I went to a nightclub where a prominent entertainer was performing. I was with a party of people who were drunk and because of the alcohol they were more prominent than the prominent entertainer. Every time he used one of his clever put-down lines someone from my party would top him with some crude slapstick.

I began to feel sorry for the prominent entertainer. Especially during his touching final number when members of my party used the slippery dance floor as a swimming pool and the club's fire extinguishers to repel the secretary-manager.

I felt so ashamed that I made it my business to apologise to the entertainer. I hate confrontation so much it took me six months to build up the courage to do it.

This meant I had to follow his show around the country for six months and like my friends, I too began to hate his reconstructed cover versions and fake adlibs. So much so that in Bunbury, just south of Perth, I grabbed a fire extinguisher and sprayed both him and his bass player during a touching final number.

If I'd have acted swiftly in Gosford, I'd have saved money. I would not have been barred from the Italian Club in Bunbury either.

The end.

Curly Hair Can Be So Cruel

I choose to start the story now.

I have curly hair and my relationship with it is like that of a parent to a rebellious teenager—it's hard to manage.

If I go to bed with a wet head, next morning my hair has got so much body it feels like a trampoline. I can bounce Weet-Bix off it. People yell out things from cars like 'Hey, big nose, take the helmet off', or 'pump up the volume, tall face'.

If you're growing curly hair there's also a difficult 'in between' period called the 'Ashtons effect'. Hair is

said to be Ashtons when it's neither short nor long
but sticks out at the sides like two gladbags full of
mashed potato. In other words, you look like you're
wearing a clown wig. I hate clowns.

When Nerida Flemming put chewing gum in my
hair I didn't mind having to shave my head to get it
out because it meant I had no curls for a while. When
this was combined with my shaved eyebrow (it got
shaved off while I was asleep on a bus during a
school excursion), I created a look that actually got
me into some nightclubs in Melbourne. I also had a
crush on Nerida. Even though there was chewy in
between us she'd touched me and that was nice.
Very tingly.

Sadly, my hair grew back into a college-boy cut. It
didn't like me having success.

Curly hair can be so cruel.

The end.

Don't Wear Tight White Jeans During the Early Stages of Courtship

I choose to start the story now.

The day I hugged Virginia in front of the nightclub was ruined by a pair of tight white jeans.

I remember it clearly. I was sitting on a brick fence. I had my legs apart and Virginia was standing in between them. My face was resting on her sternum and I could feel her heart beating. It was beating quite slowly whereas my heart was pounding. Did that mean I loved her more than she loved me? It was that very thought that broke my concentration.

I suddenly became very aware of the fact I was wearing white denim jeans and that the fence I was sitting on was very dirty. I had this vision of the boys—the ones who wore their wetsuits out socially—making fun of me for having a big brown stain on the back of my white pants. 'Hey Sandy! Your suntan's running!' or 'Sandy's got a hot sack!' That sort of thing.

I stood up and brushed the seat of my pants, making sure I faced the boys (who were standing near the doorway of the club) just in case there was a brown stain there. Then someone yelled, 'Hey look! Sandy's got a sugar banana in his pants.'

If you're male, never wear tight white jeans on a first, second or third date. You're vulnerable on both sides.

The end.

Clip-on Earrings Can Increase Your Popularity

I choose to start the story now.

I ask people to wear clip-on earrings when they visit me because it increases the possibility of them visiting me a second time.

First you need to convince your friends to wear clip-on earrings. You'll find some will be more easily persuaded than others. The reason it's important your friends wear them is that clip-on earrings tend to come off easily. There's always a chance they will have to visit a second time to search for a lost earring.

Usually people only visit me once. They find my strict domestic patterns unnerving. However, if they know their expensive clip-on earring is at my place then they have to come back, don't they?

I got the idea for clip-on earrings when I was lying still and Virginia was loving me (my favourite position). I saw one of her earrings dislodge and tumble in between my pillows—I'm rather detached during lovemaking so I see things. Later, while driving her to the railway station, I was able to innocently remark, 'Oh! Ginny! Your earring is missing. I bet it fell off at my place.'

Even though lovemaking didn't occur on the return visit (I have a slow sexual recovery rate), the potential for it to occur was there.

We found the earring and I found an effective way to get people to visit me a second time.

The end.

If Your Parents Move to a Suburb with Steep Hills, when You're in Year 11, Chances Are They're Trying to Cling On

I choose to start the story now.

We'd (Virginia, her touchy feely friend Alan and me) packed the Gemini ready to leave for Virginia's folks' hobby farm and as usual my parents didn't want me to go. They didn't have a reason—which was obvious when Mum chased the car down the street yelling, 'She isn't Italian darling' (no-one is Italian in our family)—they just didn't want me to go.

My mother's possessive display was unnecessary as it was impossible for a teenager to leave the valley suburb anyway. There are steep hills either side and as it's a new suburb there's no public transport. Unless you've got a decent car you can't leave town and because there're no jobs you can't save money, so you never buy a new car, so you never leave home.

I always knew my Gemini would find it tough getting out of town and sure enough I boiled at the safety ramp— my radiator blew. We rolled back and got Alan's Valiant but it boiled too—he did a water pump.

As I sat at home, eating one of my mother's special steak sandwiches, I understood why so many parents moved to the Valley suburb while their kids are in Year 11. It's harder for teenagers to leave home.

The end.

The More Wonderful You Appear, the More You Will Be Loved

I choose to start the story now.

My parents never had any trouble getting babysitters for me because we unashamedly crawled to them.

Once a sitter was hired, we'd immediately forward them a menu. Usually a choice between a salmon salad or beef Wellington. If they chose the latter, we would sometimes arrange for Neil (the chef at The Copper Pot) to cook it. When they weren't too busy, Neil's wife Desne would even serve the meal as well.

It was then my job to see the babysitter was kept happy until my parents returned. Be it by excellent behaviour, foot massages, or in the case of Mrs Black, going to the service station and getting cigarettes for her.

Sure our babysitters' conditions were extravagant, ie gourmet food and $70 an hour, but they were loyal to us—in a middle-class type of way. The more wonderful you appear, the more chance you have of being loved.

Unfortunately, we spoilt all the local sitters with our exaggerated wages and conditions. So much so that my parents would often go out alone because their friends couldn't attract any babysitters for their children.

The end.

Social Osmosis–The Art Of Living Through Other People's Exploits

I choose to start the story now.

Social Osmosis allows you to absorb other people's achievements without suffering humiliation.

The most common use of Social Osmosis is when a parent lives through the exploits of their child. However, you can use it in many ways.

Once I cut someone off driving in my Gemini and they signalled for me to pull over. Normally I'd do anything to avoid a street fight, but on this day I had no such fears because I was giving a Rugby League star a lift home. The League star said, 'Pull over Paul and put the bonnet up.'

I didn't tell him my name wasn't Paul but I did like he said.

The League star then went over to the man who'd verbally abused me and after 40 seconds (plus a well-placed punch) the guy came over and apologised to me.

Using Social Osmosis I experienced the power of violence and fame without leaving the car. The beauty of it was the host didn't know he'd been used. The fact that he was drunk also helped.

Sadly, the League star lived close to where the incident occurred—more or less within eyesight of the other guy. He simply followed my car and beat me to a pulp in my carport.

The end.

Always Carry a Manila Folder in a Strange Social Setting

I choose to start the story now.

When I pushed open the
door that connected the
beer garden to the lounge
bar, I knew my present for
Todd's twenty-first—
a set of chunky
stoneware wine
goblets—would not
appeal.

Before me was a dancing
scrum made up of people I once knew—Tonk, Bong,
Brainiac, The Shiftless One and Trudy (friend of
Tonk). They did not look like a chunky-stoneware-
wine-goblet crowd.

At first I thought the scrum was quite balletic as it
danced about the bar, knocking over chairs and drinks
and swallowing anyone that walked into its path.
When it moved towards me, like an animal sizing up
its prey, I changed my opinion.

Then, as if on cue, each individual in the scrum
dropped their pants and moved their buttocks in and
out with their hands to make it look like their bums
were actually talking to me.

I was kicking myself for not having a Manila folder handy so it would appear as if I was busy reading some important documents.

When entering a hostile environment, take a Manila folder so you can looked occupied if the need arises.

The end.

It's Easy to Be Humiliated So Be Prepared

I choose to start the story now.

A potentially humiliating situation is parking a car in a tight spot, during peak hour, in the city, on a hot Friday near Christmas. Pressure not only comes from other drivers who have to wait for you to park the car, but form passengers who don't want to be associated with a failure and pedestrians who may have gathered to watch a potentially hilarious debacle.

The best way to ensure you are free from humiliation is a solid preparation. Before you attempt any tight park, borrow a friend's car, drive to a sparsely populated area and practice parking it over and over. All you have to do then is wait for a hot Friday near Christmas. When that day arrives, you borrow that same car, pick up some passengers who are under the impression you've never driven this vehicle before, drive into the city at peak hour and look for a tight park.

If you've had a solid prepartion, you can almost be arrogant as you slide the borrowed car into the smallest of spaces. Even nudge the cars in front and behind for comic effect.

Preparation makes vulnerability fun.

However, do make sure your passengers have enough money to get a cab home. Chances are you'll be parked in.

The end.

Cool People May Just Be Depressed Folk

I choose to start the story now.

As a child I hated visiting people. I was always dressed in a stiff pair of denim shorts, a rope belt, a light blue Midford shirt and expected to break a record for stillness and quietness.

However, I didn't mind making these sacrifices at Vince's place. Vince was cool. He was one of the few white people who had an afro hairdo, he was eternally sullen, plus he never left the house. The perfect role model for a teenager like me.

I was drawn to him like he was some type of dark god. I'd just sit and stare at him to get a picture of what I could look like in years to come. Unfortunately I take after the side of my family that is obsessive and chatty, so it was very hard for me to emulate Vince convincingly. I'm afraid an afro hairdo doesn't suit a squat Latin gent like myself much either.

Years later, I discovered exactly why Vince appeared so cool. Many years ago Vince's wife Zelda died while they were asleep in their bed. He was so distraught he never went back into their bedroom again. Except on the day he died.

Vince was depressed rather than cool. His afro was a result of letting himself go rather than any attempt to be groovy.

I'd made a mistake.

The end.

Sometimes You Have to Stoop Low to Be Proud

I choose to start the story now.

We'd all love to do our country proud in front of millions of people. Unfortunately, the less talented among us must look in less glamorous areas to find something to be proud of.

I've only felt pride once. It was seedy but at least it's something to hang on to when I'm down. It happened at a regional Rugby League grand final. I'd gotten onto the sideline by dressing as a trainer. To look authentic I forced people to drink from a plastic bottle and ran about with a high knee action.

Suddenly the crowd roared. A winger had made a break down the sideline and I was the closest person to him. Out of all the people on the ground, I was the closest. This was a moment marked 'glory' and it had my name on it so I ran on to claim it. Sadly, the winger broke my tackle easily and went on to score. I was grabbed by two mounted police and dragged from the ground.

Nevertheless, when the policewoman said, 'It's amazing you got as far as you did. Security is tight during a final. What you did was extraordinary', I experienced pride in myself. Then she added, 'You're also stupid.' And suddenly my feeling of pride lost its gloss.

Get some pride. Even if it costs human dignity and a corked thigh from a horse's hoof.

The end.

Stubbornness Should Be Kept in Good Working Order

I choose to start the story now.

If you're an only child, you probably suffer from the Roller Door Syndrome, or what's called B & D personality. In other words, you're stubborn. When a person is being stubborn, they're said to be pulling down the roller door and sometimes the door gets stuck.

A stubborn only child is like a suburban garage. There's a space for two parents, shelves to store memories, an old filing cabinet with a lock where no one else can go, a space up the sides to store emotional baggage and no room for anything else.

If you're in a good mood you may leave the roller door up so people can see in. Mostly it's closed for private activities, and if someone interferes then down comes the roller door.

There's no cure for stubborness. All you can do is regularly service the roller on your door. Sometimes mine gets stuck and it can be quite unpleasant waiting inside a dank space for help. Even if someone does offer to help I'm usually too stubborn to accept it anyway.

Stubbornness is useful for protecting insecurities but only if your roller goes up and down easily.

The end.

PERSONAL

The Dolphin Inn
Coolangatta

Sandman
The Dolphin Inn
July 24th

Dear Virginia,

I was surprised not to get a letter from you today. I'm here for two more days. Maybe tomorrow?

I miss you. I'm still wearing the piece of leather from my belt on my finger. I'll send it down in this letter. Nobody else will touch it after me except you, so it'll be like we're actually touching. I think it's better than the ring pull which restricted the blood flow and broke the skin.

I'm having a good time, although someone did put a shoelace in my mouth when I fell asleep on the beach (which made me gag) and at the Banquet Night my wallet was stolen while I was carrying a tray of drinks. I couldn't turn around to see who it was because I didn't want to spill my new friends drinks.
Until I got a new keycard I had to sell sand packed in potato sacks to tourists from a landlocked country in Europe to get money.

How was Alan's party? I wish I could've been there. Did you sleep over? In different rooms I hope? Please don't think I'm pushy. I trust you. I just need reassurance sometimes. I miss your crooked smile and your thighs. I think that was the first thing I was attracted to. I hope you don't take that the wrong way. I'm a feminist. I just think it's important to have nice legs. And a dress that blows up.

love
Sandy. ♡

The Dolphin Inn
Coolangatta

July 26th
Dolphin Inn

Dear Virginia,

Hi Ginny. How are you? The mail comes at 4 here so I won't be able to relax until then. I <u>know</u> your letter will arrive today. I've got a feeling. I thought it might've been here yesterday. Oh well.

The trip's been good so far. I've worked a lot of things out. You know how I always seem to have problems when I ring? Well, that's passing. I now know I don't want to be a masseuse. Touching strangers is confusing. I'm rambling. Sorry. I miss you. I miss not seeing you drive past on the way to work. Tell your brother to slow down. Sometimes I don't see your face.

Lots of people remark how I'm much more handsome in the photo I show them than I am in real life. I think my clothes were more interesting when the photo was taken because I was copying your brother's taste in fashion. Please send any recent photos of your brother. I'm actually wearing his denim jacket in the photo so maybe I'm more confident and that's what comes across. Confidence is half the battle. I just wish I hadn't done the buttons up right to the top. They're ~~so~~ quite stretched and it makes me look jumbo in size.

By the way, how's Alan? Did the bike trip to the National Park go well? How many others went? Did anything funny happen?

Looking forward to your letter.

Love
Sandy

The Dolphin Inn
Coolangatta

Dear Virginia,   July 27th
                              Dolphin Inn

   I've just been to the motel office
and there was no letter. I must have
given you the wrong address.
   As I was walking back I was thinking about the night we hugged outside
that ~~████~~ club I couldn't get into. I
wish more parts of my body could have
spoken so they could have said how
much I love you too. I must admit
there's one part of my body I've been
speaking to more than usual. Someone's
trying to break into the Gemini. Hang on
a sec. Back in a minute Ginny.

   It's okay, they only took a jacket that
was on the backseat. It's the one I found
on the side of the road near Forster.
   Where was I? Oh yeah I know. I
realise I've been demanding lately. And I'm
sorry I burnt your macrame rope. I
know it's odd to be jealous of rope but
you seem to spend so much time with
that damn rope. I guess I'm just competitive. I sensed an easy victory so I burnt it.
THEY'RE BACK! THE PEOPLE WHO TOOK MY
JACKET. This is weird. They're putting
it back in the car...hang on. I wanted to
say thankyou to them. They ran away.
   Running out of things to say now...
You know how my nose clicks if you bend it
to the left and you said that was creepy.
And you won't touch it. If we get married
I ~~████~~ promise I'll get it fixed. I'll have
it straightened and shaved. You won't
have to listen to my nose click ever again.
You'll be able to touch it too. Oh well. It's
5 o'clock. What are you doing right now? Is
Alan there? Don't tell him I asked. Write soon.
                              Love Sandy x

Phone conversation at the Dolphin Inn July 28th -
between myself and Alan

ALAN: Hullo

(SOUND OF MONEY)

SANDMAN: Who's that?

ALAN: Who's this?

SANDMAN: Sandman. Alan? Did I ring your place?

ALAN: No

SANDMAN: Oh...you're at Virginia's?

ALAN: Yeah.

SANDMAN: It's after 2 am.

ALAN: So.

SANDMAN: Is Virginia there?

ALAN: Yeah.

SANDMAN: Can I speak to her please?

ALAN: She's outside cutting some bamboo.

SANDMAN: Oh.

ALAN: I'm teaching her how to make a flute.

(Sound of money dropping)

SANDMAN: I'll hang on?

ALAN: She'll be a while.

(WE HEAR GIGGLING)

SANDMAN: Is someone giggling?

ALAN: No.

SANDMAN: It sounds like giggling.

ALAN: It's the Ioniser.

SANDMAN: It sounds like giggling.

(SOUND OF MONEY DROPPING)

Alan do you know if Virginia has received any
of my letters?

ALAN: Yeah, they're good. Very funny.

SANDMAN: Did you read them?

ALAN: We both did.

(SOUND OF GIGGLING)

SANDMAN: Could you turn off the Ioniser please?

ALAN: What?

SANDMAN: It sounds like someone is giggling and
it's putting me off.

ALAN: Sorry

SANDMAN: Does she know that I'm at the Dolphin
Inn?

ALAN: Here she comes now Sandy I'll put her ...

(THE LINE GOES DEAD)

SANDMAN: Damn. Run out of coins.

Sex

I choose to start the story now.

When you're unpopular you rarely have to worry about sex. However, if it does happen, chances are you haven't had much practice and news does travel fast.

I can't stress enough the role humour can play in covering up anxieties during lovemaking. Humour is a good solid substitute for real emotion and when you're anxious real emotion can be a dangerous thing.

I like slapstick humour so that's what I try to incorporate in my sexual rituals. I often bend over and move my buttocks in and out with my hands to create a realistic character (complete with a funny voice) and that really gets my partner laughing. However, do pick a form of humour that reflects your own personality. It's easier to adlib.

For the actual sexual deed itself I suggest you use the Sandman's No Sweat Technique. Both participants take up their preferred sexual positions and barely move. It's not particularly enjoyable. It's not particularly exciting. But it does stick in your partner's mind and it's important to be remembered.

It's also hard to make mistakes when you don't move much. That's why the Liberal Party has no policies.

The end.

If You're Comfortable Losing. Stick with What You Know

I choose to start the story now.

One of the first things we compete at in life is running. If you're a slow runner, you have to develop a comfort zone for loss from an early age. It's amazing how quickly a losing mentality spreads into other areas of your life too.

I always feel more comfortable losing than winning. This was more than evident at a swimming club picnic I attended once.

As usual I came last in every thing: the sack race, the wheelbarrow race—Clive Tomkins made arms go at a speed they're not meant to operate at and I stumbled and grazed my throat.

For the sprint race I thought I should at least try and preserve some dignity. I decided to cover my inevitable loss by saying to the other competitors that my calf muscles were shortened by excessive cycling which hinders leg speed. I'm a well-organised loser.

However, at the 60 metre point of the sprint race I was clearly out in front. As the finishing line loomed I realised I might even win. Thankfully, the thought of winning made me tense, I fell over and as everyone ran past me I felt comfortable. That familiar sense of calm, which comes with constant losing, had washed over me again. As the winners got their paddle-pops I was totally at ease. I knew what to do. If I had won I would've been vulnerable and uneasy.

I would have liked a paddle-pop though.

The end.

Rehearse Loss in Advance

I choose to start the story now.

The best way to deal with loss is to rehearse it in advance.

One day I let my budgie Peter out of his cage and he flew into a hot cup of tea and his legs withered off.

I felt like he was going to die. I tried everything to keep him in good spirits, despite the fact he had to drag himself round his cage using just his beak. He had bird seed constantly stuck to his chest. Like he was wearing a sequined vest. All dressed up with nowhere to go, so to speak.

I think he felt like he was going to die but it was hard to tell. Nature's been cruel to the budgie, only supplying them with a small range of emotions to express things with. A bit like the actors on *Baywatch*.

To overcome the feeling of loss I knew I would experience when Peter finally died, I got a boiled egg, wrapped it in tissue paper, put it on a dessert spoon, carried it out into my backyard and buried it next to the lemon tree, which is a strong metaphor for life. I did this about six times.

On the day I had to bury Peter, I was able to concentrate on the boiled egg instead of his dehydrated body and withered legs. And I don't care who you are but you can't get emotional over a boiled egg.

The end.

The Difference Between Flirting and Cheating

I choose to start the story now.

As twilight turned to night Linda and I were the only two left on the oval. The others had wandered back to the cars some 80 metres away. It was obvious Linda had planned for us to be alone—she said, 'Stay Sandy stay', and she held my shirt so hard it tore.

She then placed saliva on the tip of her finger and ran it over my face, the spit made it slip over my stubble like a professional water-skier might. At the time, the significance of the 22 metre line, which ran across the oval and in between us, was not evident. But when she kissed my eyeballs, for better or worse, I stumbled forward over that 22 metre line.

For one glorious minute I lived in sin. It was beautiful. I even had to think of Nanna and Pop to avoid a sexual accident.

It was only when we walked back to the cars and Linda's husband flicked his lights on and off and sounded the car horn in short angry bursts that the significance of the 22 became apparent. That line was the difference between flirting and cheating and I had crossed it, and in three minutes' time I was going to be punched back over the line by a very angry and possessive man.

The next time I cheat I'll do it on a hockey field. At least the goal area offers more cover than Rugby League posts do.

The end.

Trying to Be Remembered is Humiliating. Trying to Be Remarkable is Painful

I choose to start the story now.

I tried for many years to be remarkable. I often told people I'd once levitated a pensioner down by a lagoon just so I'd sound extraordinary.

As you get older people need to see you being extraordinary (as opposed to just being told about it) and as a result you can become quite desperate to be remarkable.

If I ever got a lift with friends I'd get out of the car while it was still moving and act like it didn't hurt so it looked like I had a remarkable tolerance to pain. I also turned to crime to give the impression I was above the law. I stole a drum kit from a Masonic Hall. Eventually I was caught by the owner of the kit (a karate instructor), who demonstrated his ability to hurt others by cutting a Pepsi bottle in half with the side of his hand.

I now find trying to be remembered is a much more obtainable goal than trying to be remarkable. Less painful too.

I'm prepared to humiliate myself to be remembered. I'm no longer willing to endure physical pain to be remarkable.

The end.

Second Last is Best

I choose to start the story now.

When entering a new social scene, you'll be asked to give your opinion on various matters. Your response may determine which subgroup you end up in. Work on the theory that second last is best.

Answering a question that requires a response can make you anxious and cause unnatural ideas to come out of you mouth, ie dogs are more intelligent than academics. Although I still believe that theory has legs.

If you're too fast in forming opinions you'll look impulsive and only people who like danger will warm to you. You'll always be expected to live dangerously to make an impression, ie eat really hot pies, freestyle into the wall of a swimming pool for a bet. That type of thing.

To avoid making a wrong reponse be the second-last person to state your opinion. That way you get to hear what other people think first. The other advantage of being second last is when people are close to the finish of something they tend not to dwell on the second-last thing quite as much. It's first, second, maybe third at a pinch and last place that hold the interest.

Being second last is like driving from Brisbane to Sydney and stopping in Newcastle for the night. You might as well push on to Sydney. There's less pressure on the second-last thing.

I know, I come from Newcastle.

The end.

Placenames Mentioned by the Sandman

THE GEMINI

Gemini Sedan photograph reproduced with permission of Gregory's, Copyright Universal Press Pty Ltd DG 3/95

Glossary of Terms

Ashtons Effect: when your hair is neither short or long. In other words, it's said to be Ashtons.

B & D Personality (or Roller Door Syndrome): a chronically stubborn person.

Circular Breather: a person who has the ability to talk and breathe at the same time.

Conglomerate Rock Sydrome: occurs when an insecure person attaches other people's personality traits to cover their own traits.

Double Verbosist: a person who tells the same story twice.

Emotional Gecko: a person with an ability to cling on in impossible situations.

Fake Busy: the art of looking like you're doing something.

Fold Back Personality: a shy person.

Front of House Personality: an extrovert.

Harry High Pants: someone who wears their pants high.

Heat Beads: old friends.

Human Doona: a demonstrative person.

Hummingbird: person who is all arm flapping and no forward movement.

Kangaroo Tail: when you roll a towel from one corner to the other it resembles a kangaroo's tail, and when flicked it's quite lethal.

Larry Low Pants: a person who wears their pants low.

Metho: people who always ignite parties.

Morose Teenager Technique: when you're over 25, this technique allows you to turn into a morose 17 year old again.

No One Ever Comes Back from Goodbye Technique: a way of using an elderly relative (who is close to death) to emotionally effect others on a bus.

No Sweat Technique: both partners take up their preferred sexual positions and barely move.

Pilot Fish Syndrome: when a less compelling person attached itself to a more confident person for personal gain, eg the National Party.

Prairie Dog Syndrome: a chronically curious neighbour.

Sand: people who have the habit of killing-off fun. They put the fire out.

Social Osmosis: Living through other people's exploits without them knowing.

Social Red Light: a boring person at social functions.

Two Way Crack: when you can see someone's private life but they can see yours.

Ulladulla: a coastal town on the south coast of New South Wales.

Vanishing Cream: someone is said to be covered in vanishing cream when they have no charisma.